NO CUSTOMER – NO BUSINESS

The true value of ABCM

NO CUSTOMER – NO BUSINESS

The true value of ABCM

Robin Bellis-Jones and *Nick Develin*

DEVELIN & PARTNERS

ISBN 1 85355 529 0

First edition 1995
Reprinted 1996

Views expressed in this publication are the authors' and not necessarily those of the Institute or of their firm.

No responsibility for loss occasioned to any person acting or refraining from action as a result of any material in this publication can be accepted by the authors or publisher.

British Library Cataloguing-in-Publication Data
A catalogue record for this book is available from the British Library.

Typeset by York House Typographic Ltd, London
Printed in Great Britain by Hartnolls, Bodmin, Cornwall

Contents

Preface

Business life is full of TLAs – three-letter acronyms: TQM, BPR, ABC . . . People can be forgiven for a healthy scepticism about these: they are too often presented by management and consultants as a glib panacea, and seen by staff – commercial life's perennial victims – as management's flavour of the month.

Activity based costing (ABC) comes with a rash of related TLAs – including activity based management (ABM), activity based budgeting (ABB), and the garrulous four-letter acronym ABCM – activity based cost management – which is our own preference. Professor Robert Kaplan, one of the authors of the 1987 book *Relevance Lost: The Decline and Fall of Management Accounting*, said in 1992: 'Five years on, I wish we could rename the baby. It's about more than activities, and more than costing: it's about management.' Nevertheless, the acronyms are useful. They catch management's attention, and help to convey new ideas and original thinking. In no field of management is new thinking needed more than in management accounting and management information.

This book started life in 1992 as one of the Accountants Digest series published by the Institute of Chartered Accountants in England & Wales (ICAEW). The development and use of activity based techniques has accelerated rapidly in recent years, along with a much wider understanding of their potential role in the management of change, particularly in total quality and business re-engineering.

This book is published by Accountancy Books – the publishing arm of the ICAEW – in association with the Institute's Board for Chartered Accountants in Business (BCAB). This reflects enormous interest in these subjects from accountants in industry and commerce. However, our target readership is not confined to accountants: the book is aimed at managers in any discipline, and is as much about breaking down the functional barriers in organisations, and about values, beliefs and behaviours, as it is about methods and techniques.

Robin Bellis-Jones
Nick Develin

Develin & Partners
211 Piccadilly
London W1V 9LE

CHAPTER 1

The climate of change

... bump, bump, bump, on the back of his head, behind Christopher Robin. It is, as far as he knows, the only way to come downstairs, but sometimes he feels that there really is another way, if only he could stop bumping for a moment and think of it.

A. A. Milne

In 1989 a British manufacturer of pumps decided that it was no longer economic to manufacture in the UK. Alongside their own products, the company imported, badged and sold a complementary line of pumps manufactured in the Far East. The imported product sold for a highly competitive price which gave a good profit margin, and was rapidly gaining market share; the in-house manufactured pumps had low margins and were losing market share.

Fortunately, the finance director and the sales director were personal friends and extremely bad golfers. During an extended game they discovered that they both shared considerable unease about the decision to close the factory, for different reasons.

The information that underpinned the decision was based on standard costs. Manufacturing overheads, and a considerable proportion of non-manufacturing overheads, were recovered into product costs on the basis of direct labour hours. The imported pumps required very little direct labour (change the voltage, rebadge, repackage), and therefore attracted little overhead. The sales director instinctively felt that this misrepresented the true cost of the imported product, and furthermore, he believed that it was underpriced in the market.

Apart from the drastic prospect of closing the factory, the finance director was concerned about which non-manufacturing costs would need to be retained to service both the imported products and the imported replacement for the in-house product. He asked a recent graduate recruit to conduct a one-week exercise to interview departmental managers with this question: which costs would you have to keep, and which could be cut?

The result was sufficiently disturbing to delay the final decision, and led to an exercise that used activity based costing as a more rational basis for determining product costs. The in-house manufactured product turned out to cost much less than the standard costing system had alleged, and could be profitable at a much lower price. The true cost of the imported product was much higher, but it could command a higher price while still gaining market share.

This story illustrates the extent to which companies depend on standard costing systems and other management accounting information when making critical decisions – in this case, a strategic decision of great importance. It raises the question: how many such decisions in British industry have been based on such flawed information systems?

Activity based costing (ABC) acquired prominence in the late 1980s, particularly following publication in 1987 of Johnson and Kaplan's book *Relevance Lost: the Rise and Fall of Management Accounting*. That book focused primarily on product costing, but as its title implies, the issue is not only costing systems, but management accounting in general. ABC therefore embraces the whole question of management information.

We use the term activity based cost management (ABCM) to broaden the scope further, first by including the subject of customer profitability, and secondly by recognising the relationship between the theory of ABC and the management style and philosophy through which it is practised.

The purpose of this book is to critically examine traditional approaches to costing and management accounting, to describe the essential characteristics of activity based systems, and to set these in the broader context of change management.

Change

The struggle to gain competitive advantage in markets that grow more fiercely contested day by day has radically altered the complexion of many businesses: the direct costs of products and services have been cut, technology and automation have been widely adopted, and development and life cycles of products and services shortened.

These changes have caused a major shift in the cost structures of many organisations. In the manufacturing sector, direct labour costs have given way to an increasing 'burden' of overhead costs. Demanding markets and competitive capability have increased both the complexity and scope of companies' products and services in every sector, with quality becoming a critical factor in business success.

Major changes are occurring to the culture within which organisations manage themselves. The number of managers who adopt an autocratic style is diminishing, and the concepts of total quality and business re-engineering are spreading rapidly.

Amid all this change, cost accounting has largely continued to employ the techniques of the 1950s and 1960s in providing management with the basic information on which key product and investment decisions are made. These techniques recover the costs of overheads using indices such as direct labour or machine hours, which reflect production volume alone. They largely overlook the factors that increasingly drive costs, such as variety, complexity and change.

Competitive Advantage

Rarely do companies fail or lose competitive edge through lack of commitment and hard work from their management and staff. Rather, they fail because they make consistently worse decisions than their competitors. The consequences in human terms are dismal enough, but the consequences in national terms are nothing less than catastrophic. In Britain we have lost the competitive advantage we once held in industries such as motor cycles, shipbuilding, textiles, electrical goods and many more.

Governments have played their role in Britain's industrial decline, but it is too easy to blame governments for such wholesale industrial failures. One of the key differentiators is management practice, within which management information is a critical element. Good information – knowledge – is the life-blood of good decisions. We contend that management accounting, as practised today in many British companies, is failing management, often by not providing adequate information for decision making, and sometimes by providing information that is actually misleading. Nobody comes to work deliberately to make mistakes. Nobody consciously makes bad decisions. While good information cannot guarantee good decisions, poor information does guarantee poor decisions. In the absence of good information, profit is more a matter of luck than judgement, and is unlikely to be either consistent or sustained.

British companies are threatened by competitors from abroad, particularly from Europe and Japan, who *do* demonstrate both consistent success and the ability to sustain it.

Management accounts and management information

Activity based costing has been described as a revolution in costing systems. Revolutions make people nervous. There is an implication that the previous order was so flawed that revolution is preferable to steady evolution. Particularly in the case of accounting systems, such an assertion is worth careful examination, and the new approach must be tested for relevance in addressing the problems that companies face.

In recent years, traditional methods of cost accounting have been criticised both for failing to provide appropriate information and for providing misleading information, with the result that companies:

- do not know whether or not their products or services are profitable;
- cannot distinguish profitable from unprofitable customers;
- make incorrect make/buy decisions;
- initiate cost-cutting programmes that fail;
- introduce products that are certain to be uncompetitive;

- miss important investment opportunities, or make inappropriate ones;
- drive up manufacturing costs;
- design inappropriate organisation structures;
- focus on the short term at the expense of the long term;
- lack the visibility of their operations that they need to manage the business;
- maintain barriers to change.

This is a formidable list of charges. The issue here is management information: in the majority of British companies, the monthly management accounts are the only regular information about the business that managers receive. The recurring problem is that management accounts fail sufficiently to reflect the complexities of the operating environment. Managers are of course capable of making bad decisions even when they have good information, but this is no argument for providing misleading or irrelevant information. Furthermore, if the system fails to provide relevant information – that is, it *omits* what is critical or useful, managers are obliged to rely on intuition.

Dr W. Edwards Deming, the quality 'guru', asserted that the most important numbers for any business are the values that attach to happy customers, quality improvements, teamwork, pride in workmanship, and so forth. They are never known, but must be taken into account by management. The greatest danger comes from relying on 'visible figures' alone to run the business – by which he meant the financial accounts. Most management accounts are a subset of the company's financial accounts, and are expressly designed to be so. This stems from company failures in the 1930s that led governments to intervene with regulations to ensure accurate balance sheets, which in turn encouraged consistency between internal and external accounts.

The danger is therefore twofold: first, that management should rely almost exclusively on accounting information to run the business, and second that the information is itself incorrect or misleading for the purpose of making sound operating and strategic decisions.

Management trends

David Allen, the Chartered Institute of Management Accountants (CIMA) Industrial Professor at the University of Loughborough, has identified a number of management trends that are being driven by economic and competitive realities as businesses move into the 1990s. These are summarised in Figure 1.

Figure 1 Management trends

From	**To**
Stability	Discontinuity
National	Global
Tactical	Strategic
Functionalist	Generalist
Centralist	Devolved
Individualism	Teamwork
Tangibles	Intangibles
Quantity	Quality
Products	Customers
Direct costs	Indirect costs
Analysis	Synthesis
Reactive	Proactive
Accounting	Financial management
Static	Dynamic

Most organisations will identify readily with these trends, and also recognise them as a turbulent sea through which management must navigate. Intuition, emotion, and even personal experience are not enough: management needs *knowledge*. In all but the smallest companies, there exists a structural barrier to change, illustrated in Figure 2.

Figure 2 Authority and knowledge

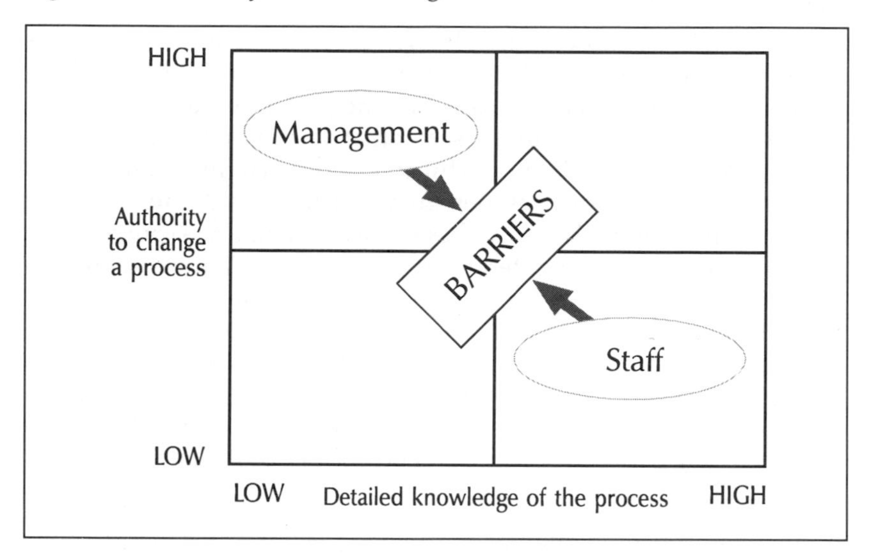

Staff, through experience, have a good knowledge of the activities within their own functions, although they normally lack visibility of the cross-functional business processes of which their own activities form a part. Even with insight, they still lack authority to make changes in the activities they undertake – only management can do that.

As an individual rises through the management hierarchy, *his or her detailed knowledge declines, while his perspective broadens and his authority to make change increases*. Ultimately, only the board have the perspective and authority to change multi-functional processes, but lack the detailed knowledge to do so effectively. Staff become victims of processes they lack the authority to change, while management become victims of their own lack of knowledge.

The nature of change

The balance of knowledge and authority in an organisation leads to the conclusion that there are three kinds of change: drastic change, continuous improvement and innovation.

Drastic change

Drastic change is almost invariably driven by an unwelcome commercial imperative – an *external* factor. Sometimes, this will be something sudden, unforeseeable and outside the control of the organisation, such as political change or a natural disaster that destroys or radically alters a market. More often, it is successful competitor activity or other more progressive change (such as deregulation) that results in declining market share or profitability. In these cases, although the source of the pain is perceived to be external, it usually results from failure to recognise the impending threat and to improve internal competitiveness to meet it. (A vivid illustration of the ability of Japanese industry to plan for, and respond to external threat, is that in the five years to 1987, Japan increased its corporate profitability by 30 per cent, and its annual trade surplus rose from US$45 billion to US$100 billion, despite its currency rising between 50 per cent and 100 per cent against all major currencies.)

Drastic change is always imposed by management, top-down. There is little or no need for knowledge of the detail when implementing such change. (Indeed, a cynic might observe that in such circumstances, too much knowledge inhibits flair, and go on to recognise that perhaps our politicians are appointed to ministerial posts on this principle.)

Continuous improvement

The second kind of change is continuous improvement. Most continuous improvement is bottom-up, based on knowledge, and depends on the existence of a culture in which people are empowered. It is usually incremental – move a filing cabinet, redesign a form, change the sequence of doing things, adapt an existing design, and so forth.

It is easy to trivialise such change, to regard it as unimportant. A powerful illustration of the power of continuous improvement is shown by a study carried out in 1988 comparing American and Japanese suggestion schemes. The Japanese system (known as Kaizen) involves all employees in making improvements. Their ideas tend to be small-scale, inexpensive to implement and concern the individual's own area of work. The results are nevertheless dramatic, as shown in Figure 3.

Figure 3 The power of continuous improvement: comparison of American and Japanese suggestion schemes

	USA	**Japan** (Private organisations only)
Total number of eligible employees	8,364,865	1,685,412
Total number of suggestions received	1,010,889	52,898,345
Number of suggestions per 100 eligible	13	3,145
Percentage of employees participating	9	80
Adoption rate	28.0%	82.5%
Average award payment per adoption	$545.68	$2.70
Average net savings per adoption	$7,663	$43
Net savings per 100 eligible	$26,870	$356,531

Innovation

The third kind of change is innovation. Innovation is often radical change, and like continuous improvement, can only flourish in a culture that encourages it. If there is a barrier of mistrust between those who have authority (the management) and those who have knowledge (the staff), such a climate cannot exist.

In the absence of continuous improvement, an organisation will decline, even if this is only relative to the competition. In this case, decline will result in the need for drastic change. Figure 4 illustrates the contrast between an organisation that combines continuous improvement with innovation, and one which is forced to rely on periodic drastic change.

Figure 4 Different approaches to change

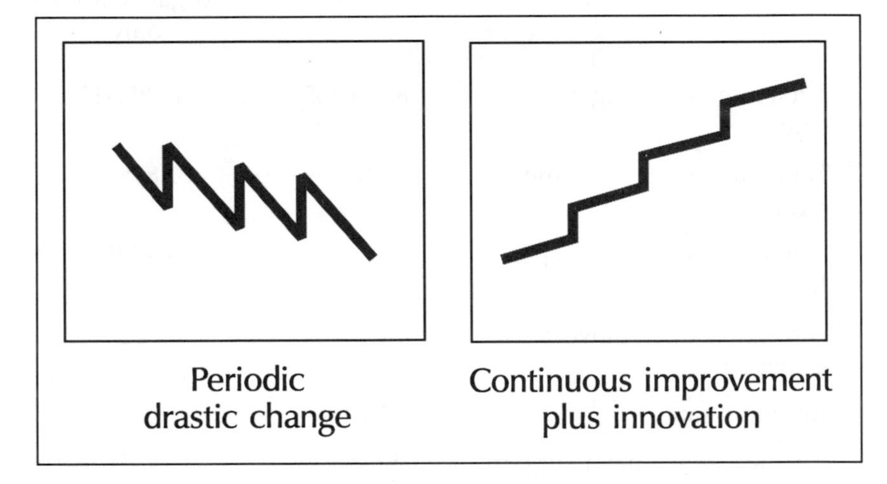

Drastic change is almost invariably destructive, unless the organisation can follow it by introducing the habit of continuous change.

The usefulness of this distinction between different types of change lies in recognising the role of management, and in understanding the barriers to change. The role of management should be to enable the continuous improvement of the processes in which their staff work, by:

- empowering staff, who have greater detailed knowledge;
- cooperating across functional boundaries;
- eliminating fear that inhibits communication;

- acquiring knowledge and understanding of those processes;
- planning, which requires the ability to predict.

If a manager is uninformed, or is misled by the information he or she receives, then personal experience, emotion and intuition are *all that remain*.

The barriers are structural. It is striking that in many organisations, individuals can hold convictions such as putting the customer first, cooperating across functional boundaries, and empowering staff – *yet behave in a way that is demonstrably at variance with those beliefs*. Why does this happen? Certainly, people do not usually do it consciously. When it happens, the result is invariably frustration and low morale.

> *A bank established a centralised unit to provide branches with foreign currency and travellers' cheques. In line with the bank's customer care programme, the unit established methods and processes to provide a responsive and proactive service to branches (anticipating demand at branch level during the holiday season, managing distribution economically using the bank's bullion runs, and so forth). Inexplicably, demand from the branches fell, and it transpired that branches were buying currency and cheques from competitors! The reason was simple: every branch and central unit in the bank was treated as a profit centre and required to make a 'contribution'. The treasury function charged the unit for the currency it 'bought', plus a margin; and the transport function charged the unit for distribution, plus a margin. The unit likewise charged branches, plus a margin. Unsurprisingly, the branches found competitors' prices cheaper, and bought from them in order to keep their own costs down, even though they took longer to supply. The accounts department spent a lot of time managing all the cross-charges and trying unsuccessfully to reconcile departmental contributions with overall profit.*

Clearly, the result was in the best interests of neither the bank nor its customers. In this case, departmental 'contribution to profit' was the dominant driver of behaviour. Branch managers knew that whatever management *said* about the importance of customer service, their own and their branch's performance would be judged by the contribution figure.

The point of this story is that nobody perceived any inconsistency between using contribution as a measure of performance, and exhortation to improve customer service. The branches simply regarded the currency unit's high prices as a typical example of head office incompetence. The currency unit saw branches as a law unto themselves. Both *believed* in customer service, but their *behaviour* contradicted that belief, and the resulting frustration was easily blamed on others.

With few exceptions, organisations are functional hierarchies. Cost centres reflect the organisation, because it is easy and convenient to account for costs on a functional basis, and to replicate the financial chart of accounts at departmental level. Figure 5 shows a typical budget statement for a purchasing department.

Figure 5 Typical departmental budget statement - purchasing department, engineering company

Description	**£000s**
Salaries	665
Associated staff costs	113
Total staff costs	778
Travel and entertainment	130
Staff restaurant	18
Telephone	14
Stationery	9
Premises – rent	65
– rates	13
Equipment – maintenance	17
– depreciation	7
Utilities	11
Insurance	5
Management fee	45
Central computer charge	27
Total non-staff costs	361
TOTAL	1,139

This statement is interesting for what it omits. It contains no mention of strategy, no mention of outputs, no mention of processes, no mention of throughput volumes, no mention of cause and effect, and no mention of the customer. In fact, it is not very useful at all. We shall return to this example in the next chapter.

Effective management of change is about management of *cross-functional business processes.*

The need

Good management information must therefore describe and monitor the performance of business processes. Since business processes consist of a series of linked activities that deliver products and services to customers, management information must:

- reflect the customer's perspective;
- provide visibility of business processes;
- explain or demonstrate cause and effect;
- identify the profitability of both products and customers;
- embody strategy;
- reflect reality;
- be predictive;
- be in the language of management.

Activity based cost management is aimed specifically at this need. Its objective is to provide the information needed to improve business processes, and then sustain the improvement, first by enabling management to focus on 'doing the right things', and secondly by providing an approach to 'doing them right'.

In the next chapter, we examine more closely the strengths and weaknesses of conventional approaches to management information in relation to this requirement.

CHAPTER 2

Conventional approaches to management information

There is only one thing wrong with Management Accounting – the word 'Accounting'

Professor Roger Fawthrop
University of Warwick Business School

In addressing the issue of information that organisations use conventionally to manage the business, it is useful to examine four main categories of management information:

- product and service costing and profitability;
- customer costing and profitability;
- budgeting;
- management accounts.

Conventional product and service costing and profitability

The strength of conventional product costing is its conceptual simplicity. A manufactured product's cost typically consists of three elements:

- material cost;
- direct labour cost;
- apportioned factory overhead cost.

This generates a 'factory gate' cost – that is, it usually excludes general overhead costs incurred in functions such as sales, marketing, distribution, computing, finance and general management. The difference between the factory gate cost and the selling price of the product is described as the *contribution* to these general overheads.

Conventional techniques generally adopt a two stage approach to allocating costs to products (or customers), as illustrated in Figure 6.

Figure 6 Conventional cost allocation

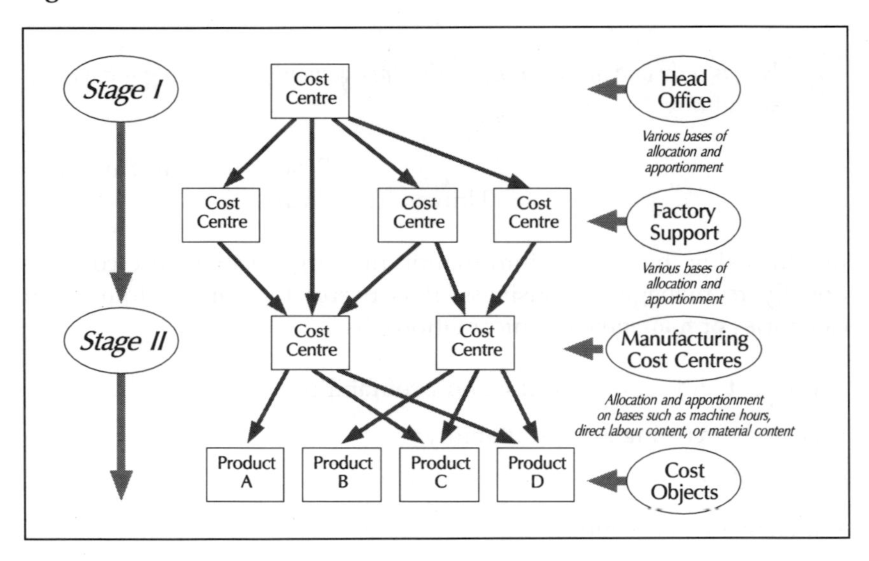

The first stage accumulates costs in cost centres. Some of these will have been apportioned from other support cost centres, such as personnel, information technology, maintenance, purchasing and head office. Once accumulated, in most companies these costs are 'recovered' into products on the basis of the proportion of direct labour they consume in manufacture, or on the basis of some other volume-related factor, such as machine hours.

In the same way, sales, marketing and distribution costs are often apportioned on the basis of sales revenue. In a company with few products, high volumes, high direct labour content and low overheads, this is likely to generate a product cost that has relatively few distortions. However, any significant complexity in the range of products, and in the customers to which they are sold, is likely to make this method inaccurate – often wildly so. The result will be hidden profit or loss.

Activity based costing, on the other hand, identifies and quantifies overhead activities, and then uses activity cost drivers as a basis for attributing these costs to products. Consider the example of two products costed using the two methods. Using the conventional method – shown in Figure 7, the manufacturing overheads allocated to Product B are four times as great as those allocated to Product A, because B uses four times as much direct labour. Consequently, Product B costs £900 whereas Product B costs only £400.

Figure 7 Conventional product cost calculation

	Product A	**Product B**	**Total**
Direct material	200	100	300
Direct labour	50	200	250
Manufacturing overheads	150	600	750
TOTAL	400	900	1,300

Manufacturing overheads = Overhead recovery rate × Direct labour

$$\text{Overhead recovery rate} = \frac{\text{Total overheads}}{\text{Total direct labour}} = \frac{750}{250} = 300\%$$

In activity based costing, the manufacturing overhead is broken down into its constituent parts, each of which is attributed to Product A and Product B according to the overhead activity actually devoted to it – as shown in Figure 8. In this instance, it transpired that Product B consumed only £220 worth of overhead, not £600 as the allocation based on direct labour had indicated. Conversely, Product A consumed £530, not £150.

Figure 8 ABC product cost calculation

		Product A		Product B
Direct material		200		100
Direct labour		50		200
Manufacturing overheads:				
Purchasing	120		30	
Product development	50		80	
Materials handling	100		50	
Inspection	180		40	
Maintenance	80		20	
		530		220
TOTAL		780		520
Product cost difference		+95%		–42%

Product B happened to be a line that used simple production plant requiring a heavy direct labour involvement. It was a well-established customer favourite, with a steady demand. Over time, the wrinkles had been ironed out of the overhead processes associated with it, and attributable overhead costs were low.

As a result of inaccuracies in the conventional method of calculation, the cost of Product A had been underestimated by a factor of 95 per cent, while that of Product B had been overestimated by 42 per cent.

Product costing is often viewed separately from other management issues. The consequences of inaccuracies are regarded as isolated and containable, influencing only product mix and possibly stock valuation decisions. However, the implications of inaccurate product costs are much wider.

There are two fundamental weaknesses of conventional product costing:

1 The use of only volume based cost drivers in production to allocate manufacturing overheads to products is inherently inaccurate. Over the last 30 years, with the introduction of new technology into manufacturing, direct labour costs as a proportion of the typical manufacturing cost chain have fallen by almost a third. Overheads have risen by almost 50 per cent. On average, direct labour accounts for only 7 per cent of total costs, and on this basis alone is suspect as a basis for allocating manufacturing overhead, which on average accounts for 25 per cent of sales revenue.

2 Recovery of general overhead costs on the basis of sales revenue assumes that the costs of product development and modification, sales, marketing, distribution and so on are equivalent for all *products*, and that all *customers* impose equivalent general overhead costs for those products.

The consequences can be serious. Inaccurate costs mean that a company may not know whether or not its products and services are profitable: where prices are effectively set by the market, low-profit products will appear highly profitable and vice versa, with the result that investment and the allocation of other resources will be directed towards the wrong products. If prices are not set by the market – for example, where cost-plus pricing is used – prices will be over- or under-stated, resulting in unnecessary loss of either business or margin.

The problems caused can run even deeper. Inaccurate product costs may cause make/buy decisions to be fundamentally flawed. How many profitable products have been subcontracted? Worse still, how many profitable industries have been lost to overseas competition as a result of decisions based on such cost information?

There are two further important weaknesses in conventional product costing, with equally serious consequences:

1 Typically, the costs of product development are related to neither product nor customer, and are recovered in the period in which they are incurred, despite the fact that the related benefits accrue over a much longer period. The consequence is artificially to depress profit in the current year. In a period of pressure on the bottom line, this is a severe disincentive to making the right long-term decisions for the business.

2 In most companies, a significant proportion of costs is driven by how the customer chooses to trade. This varies widely from one customer to another, because of the product mix they buy, and because of the way they do business. For example, customers vary in frequency and timing of deliveries, in methods of payment, in the frequency and nature of demands for product change, and so forth. Customer requirements can reach into every corner of the business.

The need is for a costing system that reflects not only the way in which overhead costs are driven by the *product,* but also the way in which they are driven by the *customer.*

Conventional customer costing and profitability

Conventional costing practice focuses almost exclusively on *product costing,* with little reference to the customer. However, the basis of competition has been changing dramatically over the last decade. If a product is not differentiated by its inherent characteristics, then it can only be differentiated in the mind of the customer by other factors. Almost universally, these are related to service and quality: manufacturing companies must now see themselves as service companies. In other words, meeting customers' needs is insufficient. Deming observed that:

> *It will not suffice to have customers that are merely satisfied. An unhappy customer will switch. Unfortunately, a satisfied customer may also switch, on the theory that he could not lose much, and might gain. Profit in business comes from repeat customers, customers that boast about your product and service, and that bring friends with them.*

In this area in particular, *perception is all there is.* This is the basis on which customers will judge the value for money of a product/service offering.

Accountancy often has a blind spot for customers, except in relation to credit control and debtor management, despite the fact that customer-driven costs can account for 50 per cent or more of a company's cost structure. A major obstacle to removal of this barrier is the presumption in the short term that all 'post-manufacturing' costs are fixed, and therefore that sales equate to profit. This may be acceptable in the very short term, but it is no way to run a business. The important thing is to understand how customer-driven costs add value to the business.

Examples of such costs incurred beyond the 'factory gate' are selling, marketing, warehousing, distribution, administration and corporate overheads. They are usually either ignored or, even worse, recovered as a percentage of sales revenue. This widely used technique implies that each unit of sales contributes equally to these costs. Nothing could be further from the truth: no two customers buy the same volume and mix of products, nor follow the same trading pattern. The variations in trading pattern are more often very wide, but are seldom reflected in how the related operating costs are attributed.

There are other more subtle complications. For example, imagine two customers who happen to purchase identical volumes of the same products in a given period. One is particularly adept at driving a hard bargain in terms of both a lower purchase price and a higher level of service. The other is not so skilled or hard-nosed. The implication of the conventional approach is that the former needs to contribute less, even though he requires more resources and effort to service. This clearly makes little sense.

Unfortunately, apportioning post-manufacturing overheads in this way is easy to do. However, it has little or no meaning, and through a combination of spurious accuracy and inability to reflect those factors which really drive cost in a business, can produce thoroughly misleading information.

Conventional budgeting

For most organisations, the annual budget is the most important instrument of managerial control over the business. In many, it is the only one. It often represents the only attempt by management to plan the future, and in many companies it becomes a surrogate for strategic planning.

It is not unusual for the annual budgeting cycle to be preceded by and to overlap the annual strategic planning cycle. The combined process is both top-down and bottom-up. The following is our caricature of the process.

- Three to six months before the beginning of the budget year, the board develops or updates the strategic plan – containing short- and long-term objectives (outputs).
- The impact of the strategic plan in the budget year is combined with a range of short-term forecasts (volumes, changes, investment, staffing, and so on) and a set of planning assumptions (such as inflation rate, exchange rates), which are communicated selectively downwards – on a functional basis.
- Functions translate the plan into short-term functional plans containing short-term (one-year) objectives (outputs).
- Functions translate their objectives into a functional budget, thereby specifying the *inputs required* to meet planned outputs.
- The budget is submitted to the finance department, which submits consolidated numbers to the board.
- Shortly before the beginning of the budget year, the board reveals that the consolidated figures were not what they had anticipated ('that is not the number we first thought of'), and that forecasts have changed anyway.
- The company enters a period of intense iterative discussion, negotiation and compromise to achieve a more acceptable set of numbers, in the hope that the tenuous link between the planned outputs and the budgeted inputs will not be severed. This process favours the articulate and politically astute.
- Discussion is cut short by pressures of year-end.
- The finance department divides the new numbers by 12, and publishes the first monthly management accounts, with headings 'Budget', 'Actual' and 'Var'.
- Management attempt to explain VARs.

Unfortunately, this description of the budgeting process is uncomfortably close to the truth in many organisations. In large companies, the process is complicated by departmental cross-charging and allocation of centrally incurred costs to departments. Figure 9 reproduces the example of a typical departmental budget statement that was shown in Chapter 1.

Figure 9 Typical departmental budget statement – purchasing department, engineering company

Description	**£000s**
Salaries	665
Associated staff costs	113
Total staff costs	778
Travel and entertainment	130
Staff restaurant	18
Telephone	14
Stationery	9
Premises – rent	*65*
– rates	*13*
Equipment – maintenance	*17*
– depreciation	*7*
Utilities	*11*
Insurance	*5*
anagement fee	*45*
Central computer charge	*27*
Total non-staff costs	361
TOTAL	1,139

The budgeting process that generates such statements has several significant weaknesses:

1 Although strategy is seen as the collective long-term intent of the board, in most companies it is usually developed on a *functional* basis: directors or functional heads are usually invited to submit their contributions to the plan. Even when functional perspectives are challenged and incorporated into a holistic view of the future, implementation is functional, through cascaded objectives.

2 The process seldom recognises *cross-functional business processes*: each department plans and budgets as though it were a separate business that operates in isolation from other parts of the organisation. The level of activity – and therefore the staffing requirement and people costs – in a purchasing department may be driven by the frequency of product changes required from suppliers that are initiated in the product engineering function. The effect of such cost 'cost drivers' needs to be understood and taken into account whatever the purpose for which costs are being calculated – product costing, customer costing, or departmental budgets.

3 It produces a statement of planned expenditure – that is, *inputs* – which are then treated to all intents and purposes as planned *outputs*. Managers are often judged on whether or not they 'meet budget', and management effort becomes focused on explaining the input variances. There is little recognition of the need to measure output, which is of crucial importance because output is what the customer receives, whether the customer is internal or external.

4 A significant proportion of the typical departmental budget is *outside the control of the departmental manager*. In the example in Figure 9, all the items in italics were recharges from other departments or central overhead allocations. They amount to 17 per cent of the total budget.

5 The rest of the departmental expenditure relates to *people and what they do* and what they consume. Hence the importance of *activities*, and the need to understand what drives activities, what the driver volumes are, the trends, and whether or not they are cyclical.

6 The process tends to extrapolate previous trends rather than reflect future requirements. There is an implicit assumption that the budget holder *knows* what activities are undertaken in his or her area, how resources are deployed across them, and what drives them. This is always a doubtful assumption, but especially so in the case of managers appointed from a different area or company. This lack of

knowledge goes unchallenged, and leads managers to fall back on what they *do* know – the previous year's budget and actual expenditure – from which they therefore derive the new budget.

Conventional management accounts

Although monthly management accounts are compatible with financial accounts, and allow costs to be analysed and tracked, they have two fundamental weaknesses as management information.

First, management accounts typically aim to provide managers of cost centres with a statement of the costs for which they are 'accountable'. This assumes that this form of management information is helpful to managers who are each running *part* of a business. In fact, the aggregate of these in the full Profit & Loss statement is only periodically and partly useful to a board and shareholders in reviewing the performance of the *whole* business. (If it were better than partly useful, investment in the stock market would be less of a gamble.)

Secondly, management accounts usually record only the costs of input, and rarely report the related outputs. They are seldom predictive, except that they record a prediction made up to 18 months ago – the budget. This has been likened somewhat cynically to a journey for which the traveller:

- estimates the distance to be travelled and the time of arrival at the destination and at 11 intermediate landmarks, without identifying the route;
- is told after each landmark how far he was from where he thought he would be, but not where he went wrong, or how to avoid making the same mistake again, or how to get back on to the right track, or even whether it was the right landmark;
- is obliged to decide where to go by looking only in the rear-view mirror.

Cost centres or departments in a company are not separate businesses, but part of the same one, and dependent on each other. Business processes that deliver service to customers are cross-functional: that is, they are only as effective as the weakest link in the chain of interdependent units.

Improvements in the performance of a business are therefore strongly related to its ability to improve its cross-functional processes. To meet this need, especially in the context of budgeting, the information supplied to management must:

- measure outputs and service levels being provided to the customer, internal or external;
- embody, reflect and support development of the business strategy;
- be predictive;
- help indicate or identify the root cause of process failure;
- show change over time;
- emphasise accuracy rather than precision;
- take into account the trade-off between accuracy and timeliness;
- enable management to focus on areas of greatest opportunity;
- show variability in repetitive processes.

There are several implications to this set of requirements. Delegated management accountability for output may be quite different from accountability for input (cost), and in the short term, they may conflict. The ability to analyse costs by product and by customer, and to understand what drives those costs, is more important than allocating costs by cost centre.

Because measures of output reflect the performance of business processes from the perspective of the customer, and because such processes are almost invariably cross-functional, *a cost centre structure may be either inappropriate or irrelevant to the successful achievement of commercial goals.*

Output measures are frequently non-financial. For example, measures of product quality or service availability are essential non-financial output measures of service which track how well the needs of customers are being satisfied.

Input costs are usually of little value on their own. However, they may be of great value:

- when they are divided by output measures to give unit costs – such as the cost per transaction;
- when they are then related to level of service – for example, to provide the cost of service levels; this can be particularly useful when levels of service can be further correlated with increased revenue or profit.

The timing of output measures should vary depending on what is being measured. It may require measuring every second or it may be annual, but there is no natural law which states that it should always coincide with the moon's orbit round the earth – monthly.

Accuracy is more important than precision. An estimate is by definition imprecise ('about a million pounds') – and often speculative ('from improved customer service'), and there is a temptation to discount such numbers for their lack of precision – to the extent, sometimes, of setting the value to zero. Precise figures are often arbitrary and valueless (it is possible to be *precisely wrong*), whereas estimates that are accurate enough to guide can be extremely valuable.

The primary purpose of management information is to measure business process performance for the benefit of both management and the staff working in the process. Much of its value depends on the extent to which it clarifies accountability, highlights cross-functional dependencies and the need for cooperation, and identifies cause and effect through the use of cost drivers.

Information that reflects the performance of the company through the eyes of the customer raises awareness of customer needs and focuses attention on both service and cost.

Summary

The only things people ever do are to undertake activities, and to take decisions that influence future activities. Activities consume resources, which have a cost. It follows that to manage cost, it is necessary to manage activities.

However, traditional management accounting information focuses primarily on the input costs, and assumes that the activities will look after themselves. Activities are not visible. How can one manage what one cannot see?

Understanding activities is more difficult than counting costs, and management information tends to concentrate on what is easy rather than on what is valuable to management. Conventional accounts do not speak the language of management: instead, they speak the language of the finance function, and describe historical inputs.

The role of management includes improving the way activities are carried out, and to what purpose. Any useful system of management information must therefore take into account the dimension of activity.

The crucial characteristic of activity is that it converts input to output. Activities are the means, not the end. However, in Western culture, managers are results-orientated, as are the management accounts. They focus on the result rather than on the means of producing it. This forces managers to concentrate on achieving the desired output, rather than on building the right conditions and circumstances that will produce it. This militates against a culture of cooperative and continuous improvement.

An individual rarely undertakes activities in isolation – hence the word 'company'. Each is dependent on others, often in other parts of the company and beyond his or her immediate influence. This interdependence has a structure: activities are linked to form business processes, which deliver products and services to customers. Management of cause and effect is at the heart of sound decisions and commercial success. It is missing from conventional financial and management accounts.

CHAPTER 3

Activity based cost management

Five years on, I wish we could rename the baby. It's about more than activities, and more than costing: it's about management.

Professor Robert Kaplan
Harvard Business School

A brief history of activity based techniques

Professors Kaplan, Johnson and Cooper are associated with the 'invention' of activity based costing (ABC). Kaplan and Johnson's book *Relevance Lost: The Rise and Fall of Management Accounting*, published in 1987, provided a powerful perspective of how conventional costing techniques in particular had failed to keep pace with the decision-making needs of managers who are faced with a commercial world of rapidly increasing complexity and change. The book became an international bestseller. Its success is a measure of the latent need which the failure of conventional costing and cost management techniques had created.

In the early 1980s, Kaplan, Johnson and Cooper had started to examine how a number of companies had identified and dealt with difficult and complex commercial decisions, with a particular interest in the contribution of management accounting information. These observations were published as Harvard Case Studies whose primary purpose was to teach the MBA students at Harvard Business School.

A pattern quickly began to emerge from their observations. The common threads to all of these case studies were the inadequacies of the existing costing and cost management procedures, and the power of activities and cost drivers as a foundation of analysis. From these case study observations came the book *Relevance Lost*, and the term *Activity Based Costing (ABC)*. It is interesting to note that when Hewlett Packard started to adopt these approaches in 1985 they called it 'Cost Driver Accounting'.

Since then Cooper and Kaplan, from their base at the Harvard Business School, have been at the forefront of researching and codifying the experience of those implementing the activity based techniques. As a result a substantial body of published material is now available (see Bibliography). Much of this has been summarised in *The Design of Cost Management Systems* by Cooper and Kaplan. This is possibly the most extensive reference book to date on the subject.

In the early days it seemed to many that ABC was primarily about costing in a manufacturing environment. This situation arose mainly because that was the focus and environment of the early Harvard case studies. However, it soon became apparent that the potential scope for the application of activity based techniques was much greater than just costing, and far wider than the manufacturing sector. We have coined the term *activity based cost management* as an umbrella for the full range of activity based techniques which support all forms of decision support information. These include:

- resource allocation decisions;
- commercial decisions;
- improving efficiency and effectiveness.

However, the nature, scope and level of detail of the information needed to support these different types of decision *are not the same*. While a well-constructed activity database can support a wide range of management initiatives, management must clearly identify its priorities so that it can deploy the most appropriate activity based approach.

Activity based techniques have been used for many years to help tackle complex business issues. Our first experience was in 1981, for both costing and cost management problems. Then, it was not called activity based anything, nor was it seen as *new*. What was evident was its power to provide the visibility and insights not available through the use of more conventional approaches.

What was originally quantified common sense has developed into a coherent framework for costing and cost management, and a robust set of methods and techniques being used by many organisations. A key factor has been the availability of cheap, accessible computing power and the development of software packages to deal with the significant number crunching needed for implementation. A number of software companies have recognised this as a significant market need and have moved quickly to produce ABC-specific PC-based software packages. The power and flexibility of these packages is improving rapidly. We discuss implementation issues in Chapter **8**.

In most organisations, activity based techniques remain a 'new' and untried foundation for management information, so they are often viewed with some suspicion and uncertainty. This uncertainty has appeared repeatedly in the results of management surveys (including our own) which show that while there is growing recognition of the weaknesses of conventional approaches to costing and cost management, there is also great reluctance to do anything about it. The difficulty is less a question of method than of overcoming cultural resistance among line managers.

Recessionary and competitive pressures, and the rapidly growing nucleus of organisations who have embraced the use of activity based techniques with demonstrable success are beginning to force the pace.

Positioning and capability – a strategic framework

In recent years, there has been something of a growth industry in mission statements, or 'vision' statements. The greatest value of such statements derives from the process that senior management engage in to develop them, not from the statement itself.

The vast majority of vision statements are carefully worded, and brief. Some are frankly negative: 'our mission is to halve customer complaints' is a real example that reminds us of the unkind description of somebody who 'aimed low in life – and missed'. Unfortunately, even positive mission statements are problematical. However valuable the process that generated them, certain key phrases are common to most of them: the company intends to be 'Number 1 / the leading . . . / the best . . . ' in its sector; the company always 'puts customers first / values them / cares for them'; people are 'the company's greatest asset / are valued'; the organisation believes in 'excellence, teamwork, quality, service, value . . . '.

While such statements are worthy and may be heartfelt by their authors, staff tend to see them at best as bland, and at worst as fraudulent – particularly if corporate behaviour flatly contradicts the sentiments: turf wars, customer complaints, redundancy programmes, and so forth.

Strategy needs to be expressed in terms that can be communicated effectively, and that provide guidance on what to do.

Positioning and capability are twinned concepts that are remarkably powerful in helping organisations to create a strategic context for process management and change. In particular, they are concepts that help grapple with the problems of how best to direct resources. They are illustrated in Figure 10.

Figure 10 Positioning and capability

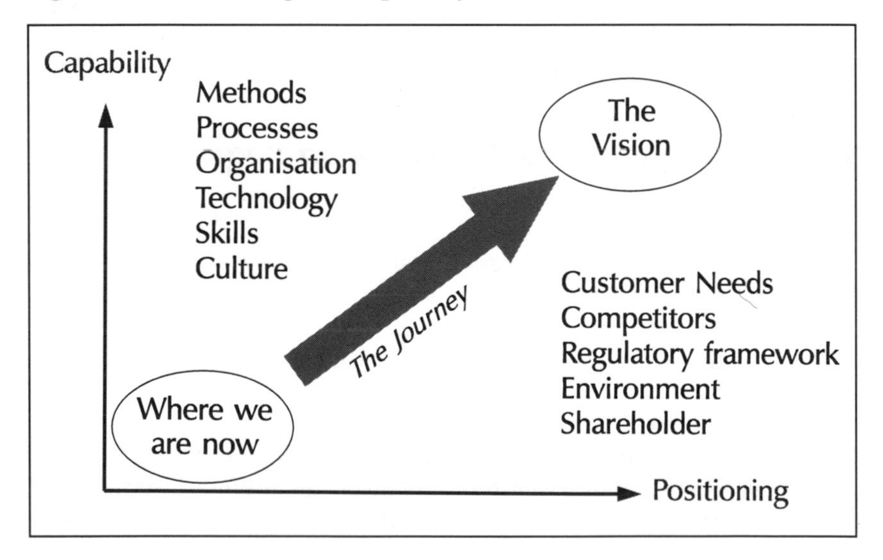

Positioning is to do with external factors such as:

- understanding customer needs, differentiated by segmentation that is appropriate to the market;
- understanding competitor initiatives;
- anticipating changing legislation;
- responding to environmental and macro-economic influences and constraints;
- determining the business's financial needs and constraints, and meeting the needs of shareholders.

Capability is to do with internal factors such as:

- the effectiveness of key business processes;
- the efficiency and cost-effectiveness of methods and procedures;
- the technology that the organisation must master;
- skills and competences;
- culture – attitudes, style, values, beliefs and behaviours.

Changing an organisation's positioning and capability can be seen as a never-ending journey towards its vision of where it would like to be. The vision should therefore be a clear statement of how the organisation wishes to position itself in relation to its customer base and competitors, and of how it intends to develop its capability to do so.

Some companies focus inwards, developing their capability without understanding what their customers need or what their competitors are doing. Others focus outwards, positioning themselves so as to set objectives their business processes are incapable of meeting and creating customer expectations they cannot satisfy.

Positioning and capability are inextricably linked; organisations must work on both at the same time. In principle, capability is developed to deliver the organisation's planned positioning, but often a specific capability (such as a manufacturing process, or a technology) will enable it to create a differentiating position in a market.

It is seldom possible for an organisation to make the transition to its 'vision' directly. The journey is in two stages, illustrated in Figure 11.

Figure 11 Stages in the journey

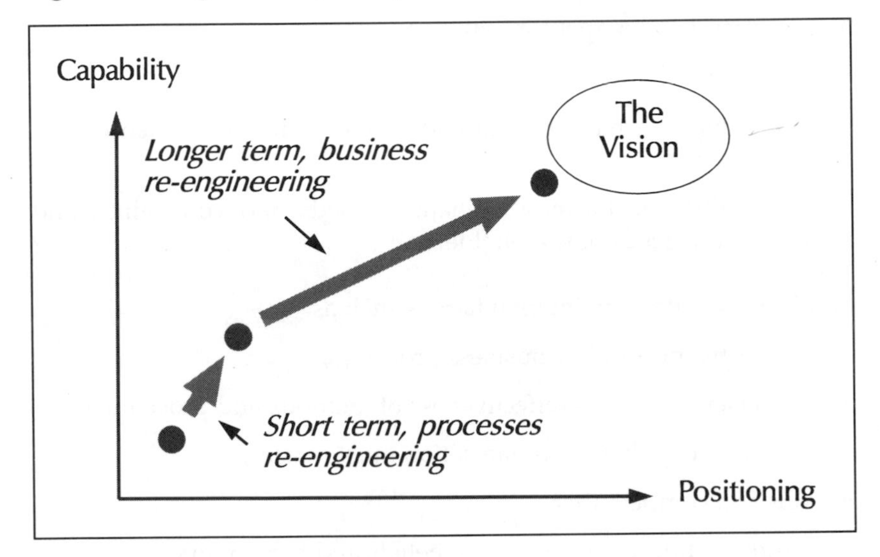

The first involves the elimination and reduction of waste in current processes, and removing the barriers to cross-functional management of business processes that are ingrained in functional organisations. The result of this stage is to improve *short-term* effectiveness so that the company can meet *current* market needs. This first stage can be described as *business process re-engineering*.

The second stage involves changing capability to meet the *long-term* positioning of the business. This requires both market research and innovation by senior management: the resulting positioning may demand significant change to internal capability, and therefore substantial redesign of the whole business – processes, organisation, competences, technology and culture. This stage can be described as *business re-engineering or redesign*. If market, competitor and shareholder constraints allow time for this change, it is best achieved through continuous improvement and innovation, rather than drastic change

A framework for activity based cost management

Positioning and capability provide a powerful framework for strategy, by helping management to focus on *what needs to be done.*

Activity based cost management has a vital role to play in supporting a company's development of its positioning and capability. The basic premise is that *activities consume resources, and convert them into output.* Business processes consist of activities that are linked across functional boundaries to deliver products and services to customers. It is therefore critical to understand the drivers of activity throughout the business, both to improve the effectiveness of the activities and processes, and to enable overhead costs to be allocated on a rational basis to products, customers and channels: this is the basis of ABC.

Activities consume resources, and therefore cost. Costs are the *consequence* of resource decisions, and income is the *consequence* of linked activities – or cross-functional business processes. The requirement is therefore:

- to improve resourcing decisions as the means of managing costs;
- to improve processes as the means of improving both internal effectiveness and customer service.

Understanding activities and what drives them is the starting point for providing management information for many different purposes. This is the basis for the ABCM framework, which is shown in Figure 12.

Figure 12 The ABCM framework

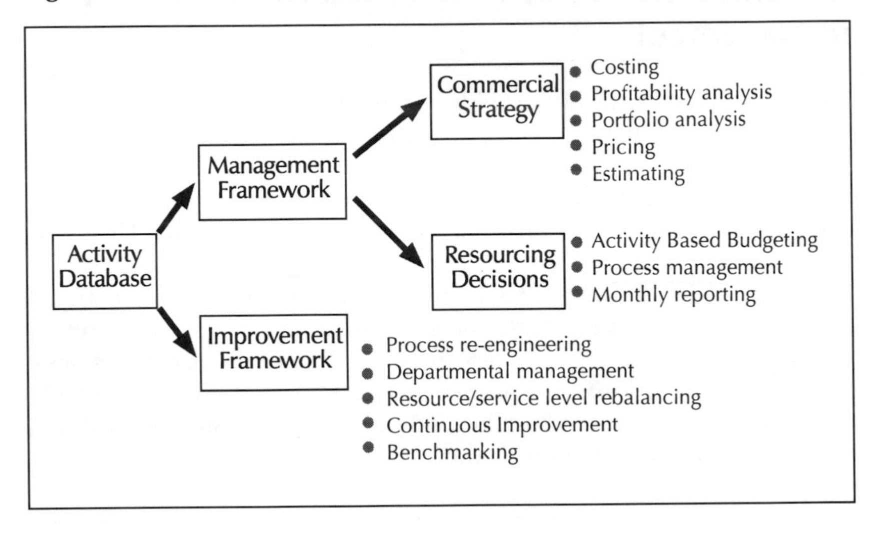

The framework recognises two main types of management requirement: support for day-to-day management of the business (the 'management framework'), and support for improvement initiatives (the 'improvement framework').

Within the *management framework* there are two key types of requirement:

1 *Profitability management*, which includes costing of products, customers, sales channels, and so forth; profitability analysis; portfolio analysis to support product and customer mix decisions; support for pricing decisions; and modelling activity, usually in support of marketing initiatives.

2 *Resource and performance management*, which includes changing the levels of activity (and therefore resources) in response to volume and service level changes; measurement of the effectiveness of cross-functional business processes; regular information to support management accountability; and planning and budgeting on the basis of activity costs and cost drivers.

By contrast, the *improvement framework* provides the basis for *change* initiatives, which includes incremental improvement, radical process re-engineering/redesign, major resource rebalancing and systems change. These three types of management support link into the positioning and capability model as shown in Figure 13.

Figure 13 ABCM support for positioning and capability

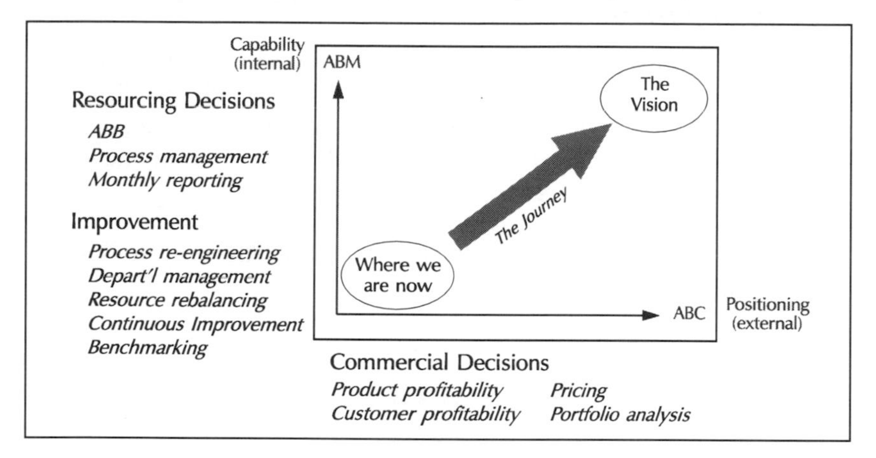

Linking the ABCM framework with positioning and capability in this way provides a coherent means of identifying the purposes for which an activity data base is to be used.

For some organisations, the critical issues may concern positioning – providing better information on matters such as product and customer profitability, portfolio or mix decisions, and pricing. We discuss positioning issues in Chapter **6**.

For other organisations, capability issues may dominate, driving the need for effective allocation and management of resources, or providing visibility of processes and activities to support improvement initiatives and in managing a change culture. We discuss capability issues in Chapter **7**.

Critical points in planning ABCM

Because the use of activity analysis has such a diverse range of application, it is important to be clear about three things at the outset:

1 the purpose of the exercise;

2 ownership of the process and its results;

3 analysis and decision timescales.

Clarity of purpose

The design of an activity database is strongly dictated by the initiative it is there to support. An activity database designed specifically to provide a basis for the improvement of the efficiency and effectiveness of an organisation will require different levels of detail from one suited to costing and resource allocation.

The framework we have described above provides the basis for clarifying the purpose.

Ownership by line management

Management must own the ABCM model, what goes into it, what it is there to achieve and the corresponding results.

A recent study by Cooper and Kaplan in the United States examined eight organisations which had implemented ABC. Four of those selected regarded their implementations as being an outstanding success; the other four were regarded as disappointing. The purpose of the study was to identify the main determinants of success and failure.

The study highlighted several key factors that differentiated outcome, none of which related to technical issues. The three most important factors were:

1 The need for a senior management project champion, who was prepared to lend it active and visible support.

2 The need to carry the management team as the project developed.

3 The need to ensure that management takes the results seriously and 'uses them in anger' to support commercial and resource management decisions.

None of these differentiators of success is specific to the implementation of activity based projects, but without them even the best of efforts can cause an ABCM project to fail. Such failure is not the fault of ABCM, but of poor project management.

Analysis and decision timescales

In the long term *all* costs can be 'varied' by management, while in the short term, the opposite is true. Three issues have to be considered:

1. The first relates to the *type* of management decision which is to be supported by the ABC model. For example, in respect of product and customer portfolio decisions one should focus only on those activity costs which are avoidable, or are capable of being varied by management as a consequence of the related decision. By contrast, management may prefer that pricing support information be shown on a fully absorbed basis, albeit one which is activity based.
2. The second is to understand the *timescale* of the decisions which will be supported by the activity based model. For operational decisions, which have a short-term impact, relatively few costs can be varied. However, for long-term strategic decisions, far more costs can be varied.
3. The third is to understand the degree to which management is *prepared* to manage its resource base. This is as much about management style and priorities as their perception of the commercial imperatives facing the organisation. In this respect no two management teams are the same. Understanding management's perspective on this issue and reflecting it in the structure of the ABC approach is a key influence on whether the resulting model is seen by management as credible.

Summary

Positioning and capability provide a useful strategic framework for examining the potential benefits of activity based cost management.

Understanding activities, their costs and what drives them provides a powerful basis for supporting commercial, resource management and change management decisions.

In planning ABCM, clarity of purpose, ownership of the results and decision timescales are critical factors.

CHAPTER 4

The principles of ABC

Concepts and tools, history teaches us again and again, are mutually interactive. One changes the other. That is now happening to the concept we call a business and to the tools we call information. The new tools enable us – indeed, may force us – to see our businesses differently.

Peter F. Drucker

In Chapter **2** we discussed the key weaknesses of conventional approaches to costing – the most significant of which is that they fail sufficiently to reflect reality. By contrast, activity based cost management is based on the following principles:

- Costs represent the expenditure incurred in acquiring *resources*.
- *Activities* use or consume *resources*.
- Activities are linked across functional boundaries to form *business processes*.
- The amount of activity consumed, and therefore the cost, is dictated by the appropriate *cost driver*.
- *Activity costs* are linked to *cost objects* by means of the appropriate *cost driver*.

Customers purchase products and services, which are produced by activities, which consume resources, which can be expressed in financial terms. However, not all activities can be usefully linked to objects such as products or customers: some costs (resources) are present in a company to sustain the very existence of the organisation itself, both now and in the future, and these are called infrastructure or sustaining costs. The general ABCM model is illustrated in Figure 14.

COPY?

14 The ABCM model

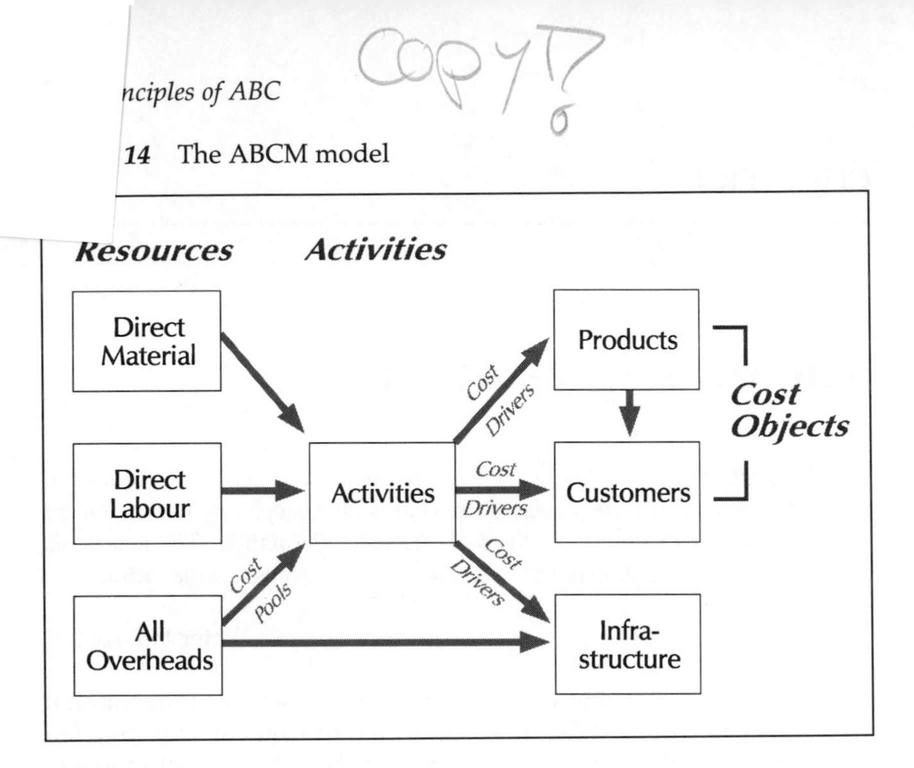

Resources

The most important feature of the ABC model is that it describes resources that are *used by activities*. In contrast, conventional accounts describe resources that are *supplied*. The difference between the two is *excess capacity*. Thus:

Cost of Resources Supplied = Cost of Resources Used + Cost of Excess Capacity

This has been described by Kaplan and Cooper as the 'fundamental equation of Activity Based Costing'. It is illustrated by means of the example shown in Figure 15.

Figure 15 ABC income statement

Example of ABC Income Statement			
	£	£	£
Sales			20,000
Less: Variable spending			
Materials	7,600		
Energy	600		
Short-term labour	900		9,100
Contribution margin			10,900
Less: Activity expenses	**Used**	**Excess**	
Direct labour	1,400	200	
Machine run-time	3,200		
Purchasing	700	100	
Receiving/inventory	450	50	
Production runs	1,000	100	
Customer administration	700	200	
Engineering changes	800	(100)	
Parts administration	750	150	
Total Activity expenses	9,000	700	9,700
Operating profit			1,200

The excess capacity should not be treated as a 'variance'. The issue is to focus management attention on the action to be taken in relation to the excess capacity *in the medium to long term*. In the short term, it is not usually possible to reduce excess capacity – labour is not variable in the short term – while shortfalls in capacity must be addressed by overtime, temporary labour, subcontract or labour flexibility.

The temptation to treat excess capacity as a 'variance' has another implication, illustrated again by Kaplan and Cooper by means of the example in Figure 16.

Figure 16 Measuring the costs of using capacity

Department with periodic operating costs of £120,000		
	Activity volume (units)	*Unit cost (£)*
Theoretical capacity	6,000	20
Practical capacity	5,000	24
Budgeted volume	4,000	30

The department's theoretical capacity of 6,000 is just that: theoretical. Because demand may be seasonal, it is more useful to base unit cost on practical capacity – that is, the department's capability, which in this example is 5,000, giving a unit cost of £24. However, if the budgeted volume is only 4,000, the unit cost should *not* be revised to £30 to avoid an 'unabsorbed cost': the issue that requires management attention and action is the *excess capacity*, and this is not addressed by hiding it behind a different unit cost. Imagine that the *actual* volume turns out to be only 3,000 (the probable consequence of a higher price based on the higher unit cost of £30): the unit cost would then have to rise to £40, which would result in yet lower volumes – a 'death spiral'.

Focus on such volume variances has another drawback: it tends to lead to the belief that once a variance is eliminated, an objective has been achieved. This confuses inputs with outputs, so that managers are judged on whether or not they 'meet budget'. The purpose of a budget is to help management decide what resources to *supply*, and once this decision is made, the need is to understand how such resources are used and the resulting capacity issues. Activity based costing meets this need. The budget does not constitute the 'correct cost', and meeting budget does not necessarily imply success. Taking no action beyond meeting budget is a form of management complacency akin to the 'if it ain't broke, don't fix it' syndrome. Not 'fixing' something that works precludes the possibility of (continuous) improvement.

Activities

People can only ever undertake activities, which includes making decisions which subsequently affect future activities. In describing the operating environment in terms of activities we are describing the world in terms that everybody can recognise: the language of management.

Activities convert inputs to outputs – that is, all activities should have a cause and a consequence. If they do not then their existence and purpose should be closely questioned.

In the ABCM model, activities are normally human activities, such as selling, designing, purchasing, but not necessarily so: they may be carried out by equipment.

All activities have an input and an output. In the example shown in Figure 17, the activity of *purchasing* is initiated by the receipt of a purchase requisition from another department (its *input*), and results in a purchase order which is sent to a supplier (its *output*).

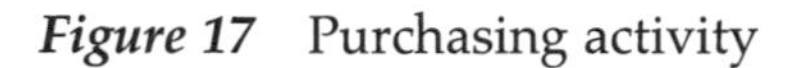

Figure 17 Purchasing activity

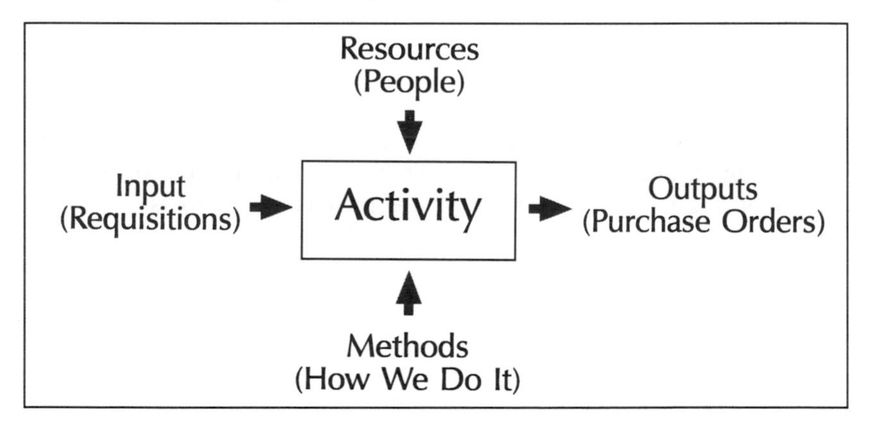

The cost of an activity is made up of the cost of all the resources the activity consumes. This includes people costs – salaries and related expenses – allocated on the basis of the proportion of time people spend on the activity, as well as other expenses such as equipment, travel, entertainment and space. What is included will depend on the time-scale and nature of the decisions to be made.

The rate at which an activity consumes resources depends on three factors:

1 Its *frequency*: this is determined by the activity's *cost driving factor* (see below). All cost driving factors have a related volume: the purchasing activity may be driven by the number of purchase requisitions.

2 The *method* used to carry out the activity: for example, the cost will vary depending on the level of automation used.

3 The *service level* required: the higher the level of service, the higher the unit cost, and this is exaggerated when there is variability in the demand for the activity. Capacity may be needed to handle peaks, leaving excess capacity in the troughs.

Note that for purposes of costing products, customers, channels and so on, costs are calculated on the basis of a *given* method and service level. An ABC cost model should be able to model the effects of changing methods and service levels, but the definition of cost drivers should be restricted to the activity's frequency.

Business processes

A business process is a series of activities, usually in different departments, which link together to deliver value to an internal or external customer. Figure 18 illustrates a typical purchasing process.

Figure 18 A typical purchasing process

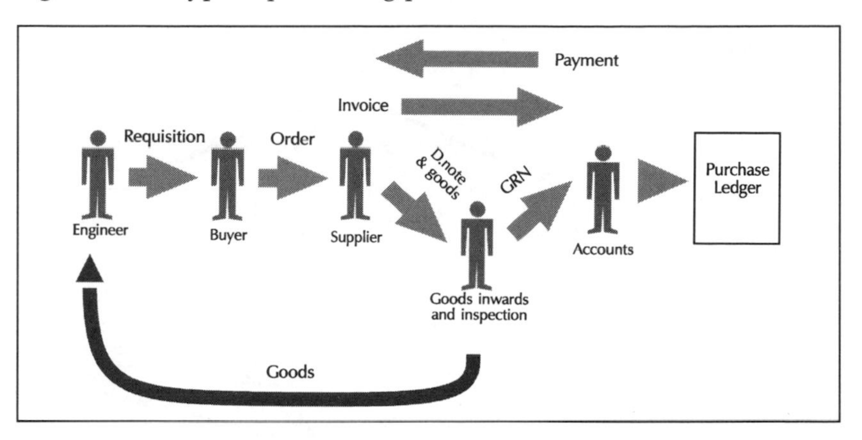

A purchasing process includes not only the activities of the purchasing department, but also linked activities in other functions, such as assessing requirements, requisitioning, quality assurance, supplier payment and purchase ledger.

Organisations are managed as functional hierarchies as much as anything because financial and management accounting systems are structured on the basis of departmental cost centres. Although this helps accounting for expenses, it provides little or no visibility of how costs are driven, which is invariably related to business processes. Cross-charging does not resolve this problem.

Cost drivers

A cost driver identifies the frequency with which an activity must be performed and therefore the amount of resources it consumes.

Cost drivers have a dual role. First, a cost driver determines the volume of the activities in a process. For example, the number of product modifications, represented by the number of engineering change notifications (ECNs), can be the cost driver for many different activities throughout the business, from product development through to purchasing and to the maintenance of bills of material. The term *cost pool* refers to the aggregation of all the activities which are driven by the same cost driver. Figure 19 illustrates an example of cost drivers and cost pools.

Figure 19 Cost drivers and cost pools

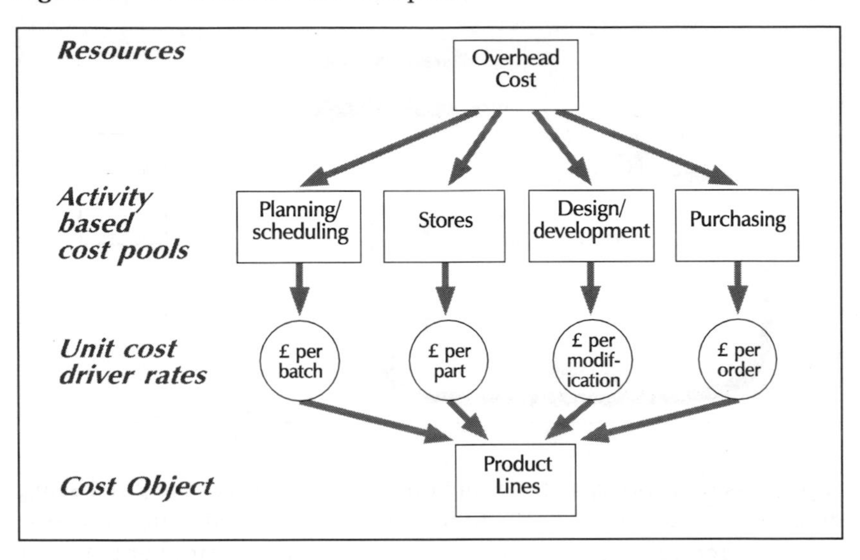

Secondly, cost drivers characterise cost objects (usually products or customers): for example, the need to produce 1,000 items could be met either by producing one batch of a thousand involving only one machine set-up, or by producing 10 batches of 100, on 10 different occasions. The set-up effort involved in the single large batch will be one-tenth of the set-up time of 10 batches of 100.

In this example, volume of output is clearly not the driver of the set-up activity, whereas the number of set-ups is, and should therefore be the cost driver of the setting activity. Similarly, the pattern by which a customer chooses to order a given quantity of product in a given period can be influenced by the number of orders placed. In neither of these cases does a conventional costing system reflect operating behaviour.

Cost objects

The purpose of ABC is to assign costs to *cost objects*, which may be products or customers, but may also be, for example, product or customer groups, markets, sales or distribution channels, projects, and so on.

Cost objects can be characterised in terms of their cost drivers, illustrated in Figure 20.

Figure 20 Cost drivers

- In 1992, to meet the demand for dinner plates we :
  - *used 20,000 kg of clay*
  - *used 90,000 litres of water*
  - *300 hours of direct labour*
  - *scheduled 20 batches of product*
  - *raised 10 purchase orders*
  - *used 400 hours of kiln oven time*
  - *inspected 45,000 fired items*
  - *rejected 350 fired items*
  - *packed 2230 boxes of finished items*
  - *loaded 120 pallets*
  - *despatched 120 trunkers of finished product to stock warehouse*

- In 1992 J. Bloggs Ltd. :
  - *purchased 3,200 dinner plates*
  - *purchased 400 seconds*
  - *placed 12 routine orders*
  - *placed 2 emergency orders*
  - *took 14 deliveries*
  - *had 12 invoices*
  - *paid 3 weeks late on average*
  - *used merchandising materials*
  - *had 6 calls from our merchandisers*
  - *had 15% discount off list-price*

Summary

The principles of ABCM are straightforward. Because *resources* (people and equipment) perform *activities*, they can be allocated to *cost objects* (products and customers) on the basis of the *cost drivers* of those activities.

ABC measures the costs of resources used, rather than the costs of resources supplied, the difference being excess capacity, which requires medium- to long-term management attention. Because activity based costing focuses management on medium- to long-term decisions, there is seldom a need to report activity based costs monthly. Furthermore, the level of accuracy required has to be consistent only with the nature of the decision to be made, rather than meet accounting levels of precision.

CHAPTER 5

Reflections of reality – the practicalities of ABC

A young frog saw snakes devouring many of his relatives. Aiming at survival, he went to visit a wise old owl. 'What can I do to avoid being eaten by a snake?' he asked. The wise old owl pondered and then advised, 'Fly away'. The frog was delighted by this simple solution – until he tried to flee from an approaching snake. 'Sorry,' said the owl as the frog disappeared down the snake's gullet, 'I only deal in concepts, not reality.'

Chinese proverb

Having described the basic principles of ABCM, in this chapter we deal with the practical issues of analysing costs in the general ledger, identifying activities and their cost drivers, and quantifying them. We also examine the all-important distinction between the different types of activities and cost drivers and the implications this has for subsequent analysis.

Understanding the general ledger

In many organisations, the general ledger is more an obstacle to the understanding of costs than a help. At worst, the structure has not been reviewed for years, and bears little resemblance to the current structure of the organisation; expense headings have proliferated beyond any valuable level of detail and groups of them are inconsistent in different parts of the organisation; and the discipline and accuracy with which ledger entries are made can also be very poor.

Interdepartmental cross-charging may be rife, often as a consequence of rewarding managers by the extent to which they 'achieve budget'. This can make it very difficult to distinguish between real expenditure and 'wooden dollars'. Finally, managers may feel no ownership for the expenditure details which are accumulated against their cost centres in the general ledger.

While the state of the ledger may satisfy the auditors for the purposes of financial accounting and reporting, it may require considerable effort if it is to support an activity based model, particularly one that requires to be refreshed periodically and deliver more than relatively simplistic results.

The general ledger is the first minefield and careful attention to it at an early stage can pay significant dividends.

Understanding the organisation and its cost structure

The first step is to divide the organisation up in such a way that the costs extracted from the general ledger are compatible with how people in the organisation are grouped. This makes it easier to relate the cost of resources incurred with the corresponding activities which staff perform.

If a particular cost centre is large and encompasses a wide variety of substantive activities, it is useful to divide staff into groups, each of which has a more limited and definable purpose. The costs of the cost centre may then be directly associated with each of these groups. If the cost centre structure of the general ledger is entirely compatible with the groups that are defined then this can greatly facilitate the automatic download of general ledger data for periodic update of the activity based cost model. If this is not the case, there may be a case for some restructuring of the ledger.

Identifying and collecting activity data

Collecting activity data is not difficult. The practical issue is the level of detail needed, and this depends on the purpose of the exercise.

There is an important distinction here between activity based costing (ABC) and activity based management (ABM). The purpose of ABC is to identify the cost of products, services, customers, and channels. These costs can then be set against the corresponding revenue in order to assess either profit or contribution. In the public sector, level of funding, or resource allocation, may be alternatives to revenue – for example, ABC may be used in the Ministry of Defence to determine the cost of training naval ratings; in a local authority to cost the delivery of public services; or throughout the sector to measure the cost of a service that is to be market tested.

The purpose of ABM is twofold: first, to quantify the cost of outputs throughout the organisation so that management can assess value for money. Second, it identifies which activities fail to add value, and therefore the level of opportunity from seeking out and eliminating the root causes of waste.

The constraining factor in an ABC exercise is *not* the collection of activity data. For costing and resource management purposes, an activity can have only one cost driver (otherwise it would be impossible to calculate the cost per unit cost driver). It is usually *the cost driver volumes which are difficult to obtain*. The constraint on obtaining the cost driver volumes therefore becomes a constraint on the level of detail at which activities are defined for costing purposes. Too much detail is also impractical. There needs to be a balance between the amount of effort needed to collect the data, and the credibility of the results.

> *In 1983 the Havant plant of IBM (UK) attempted to implement an activity based approach to resource management in an attempt to achieve greater ownership of both costs and cost drivers by management. The initiative foundered mainly because those managing the project were unable to contain the level of detail at which activities were defined, resulting in a cumbersome database, spurious accuracy and low levels of ownership by line management. This set back the cause of activity-based techniques at the Havant plant by almost five years. Since then a more focused and successful implementation has been achieved.*

In Chapter 7, we discuss the use of activity data in the management of change, where it is important to identify whether or not activities add value: for this purpose, more detailed activity data collection is needed.

The framework shown in Figure 21 provides a useful method of ensuring that the correct level of activity detail is identified uniformly across an organisation, consistent with the purposes for which the activity and cost driver data will subsequently be used.

Figure 21 Levels of activity detail

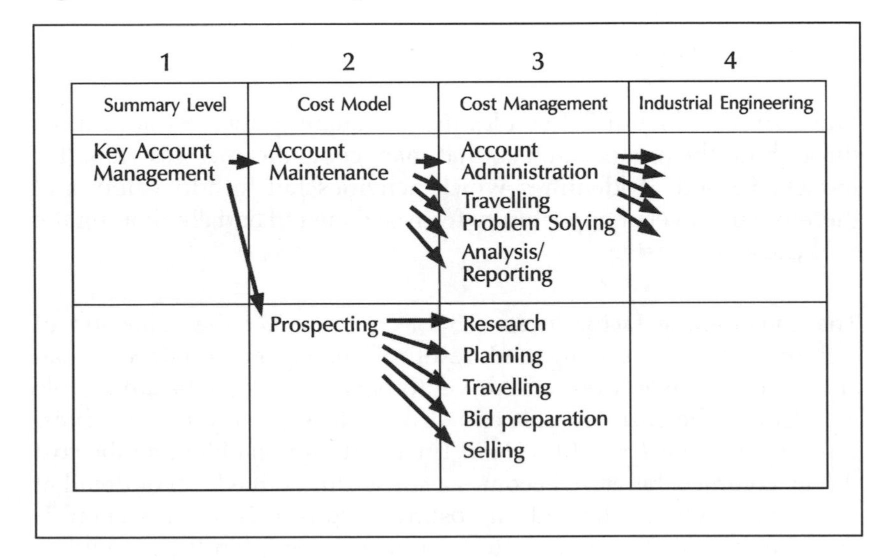

There are four levels of detail at which activities can be defined:

- *Level I* is a summary level – only appropriate to high-level reporting of process or functional costs.
- *Level II* is best suited to the understanding of activity/cost driver behaviour for the purposes of costing exercises and resource allocation decisions.
- *Level III* identifies subactivities in sufficient detail to determine whether or not activities add value (we discuss the principle of 'core, support, and diversionary' activity in Chapter 7). Associating cost drivers with each of these sub-activities is very work intensive and only worth it if unusually high degrees of precision are required: the effort required is in collecting the cost driver volume data, not the activity data.

- *Level IV* provides further detail, which is normally only appropriate for industrial engineering, work study and organisation and methods work.

Activity databases for improvement purposes

If the main purpose of the activity database is to identify opportunities for improvement, Level III data can be collected remotely by asking departmental managers and supervisors to complete forms allocating their staff's time to main and subactivities. Even in large organisations this can be done in a short space of time, and the accuracy of the data produced is almost always sufficient for evaluating and prioritising opportunities for change. We discuss this in further detail in Chapter 7.

Activity databases for commercial decision making and resource management decisions

For commercial decision making and resource management decisions, data should be collected at level II. However, for these purposes, *it is essential to understand both activities and their respective cost drivers together.* In our experience this can only be undertaken properly through face-to-face dialogue with those who are best positioned to understand such relationships.

This process of activity and cost driver definition can generate genuine understanding of the cost structure of an organisation and of what influences it. Attempting this remotely, without dialogue, creates an activity and cost driver database which lacks consistency, and which has little credibility with those whose decisions will be affected by the results.

In many organisations there is an almost tangible antipathy between cost centre managers and the finance function – respectively 'financial illiterates' and 'bean counters'. A major benefit of this form of data collection is that, often for the first time, these barriers are eroded by the dialogue that is central to the process. Critically, it engenders an ownership of cost information among line managers.

At the heart of a well-constructed activity based model is a strong cause-and-effect relationship between each activity and its cost driver.

Understanding the strength of this causality is particularly important to the credibility of the results with management.

A recent Develin & Partners survey demonstrated that the majority of UK companies recover production overheads on the volume bases of labour, material, and/or machine hours, or as a percentage of revenue. Other overheads are recovered on the basis of sales volumes or revenue.

This does not reflect reality. For over half the companies surveyed, overheads accounted for more than 50 per cent of total operating cost. Furthermore, overhead recovery rates are not just increasing, but appear to be accelerating. It is therefore not surprising that management and accountants are increasingly concerned about the diminishing accuracy of product costs.

The problem occurs because conventional costing systems allocate overhead costs on the basis of volumes alone, without recognising how overhead costs are driven. An ABC model overcomes the problem by reflecting the cause-and-effect relationship between activities and the products, services, channels and customers they support. This cause-and-effect relationship is illustrated in Figure 22.

Figure 22 Cause and effect between activities and products

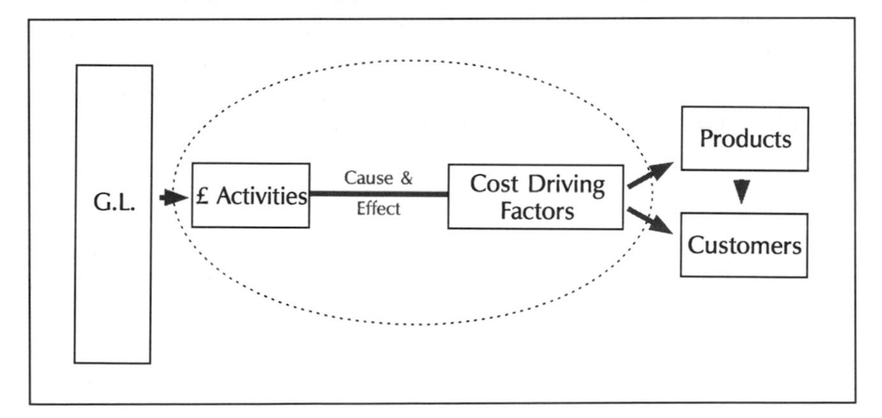

An activity based cost model should recognise that all overhead activities fall into one of four categories, *each of which exhibits a different strength of causal relationship between an activity and its cost driver*:

1 front-line activities;

2 support activities;

3 sustaining activities;

4 infrastructure activities.

These are illustrated in Figure 23.

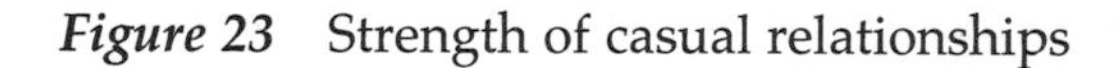

Figure 23 Strength of casual relationships

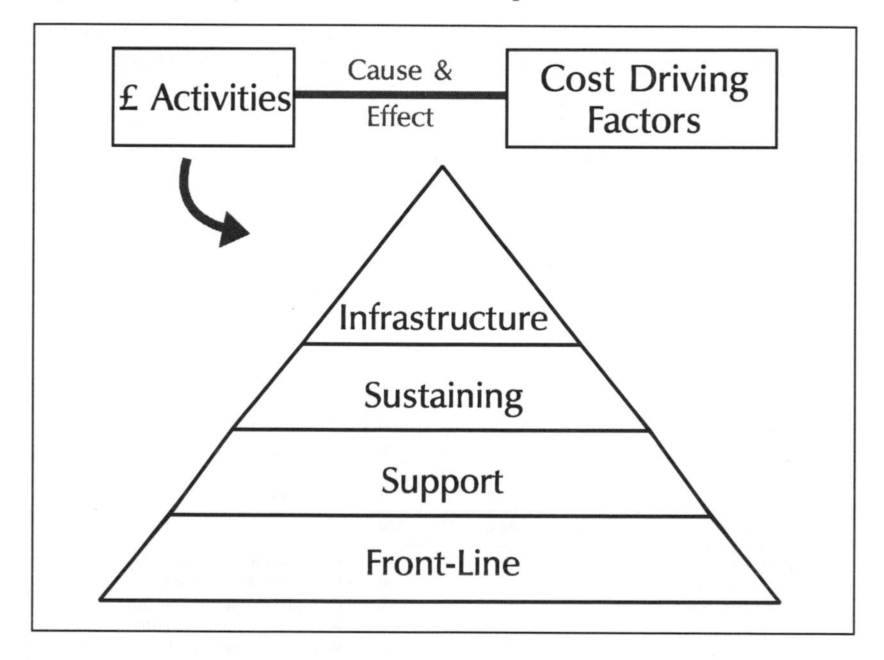

Front-line activities

Front-line activities have a strong cause-and-effect relationship through their drivers with the objects being costed. For example, the activity of processing a customer's order may be driven directly by the number of orders the customer places, which will in turn dictate the share of the cost of that activity attributed to that customer.

Support activities

Support activities have an *indirect* cause-and-effect relationship with cost objects. Examples of support activities are staff recruitment and training, payroll processing, and management. Within the ABC model their costs are normally *reallocated* to front-line, sustaining or infrastructure activities through *secondary* cost drivers, such as the number of employees, or the number of square metres of office space. In this way, the *full* cost of employing people and of the activities they undertake becomes visible to management -- often for the first time.

> *As part of its ABCM study a company initially sought to understand the cost of employing each grade of staff. Its starting point was the departmental budgets. However, as the table in Figure 24 shows, when some of the support costs of employing staff were taken into account it exposed the true cost of employing staff – almost double the cost that had been previously recognised by management.*

Figure 24 Full cost of maintaining staff

(example data)

US Dollars 000s	Clerical	Analysts	Accountants	Manager	
Personnel Cost	55	69	92	129	- Salaries, Soc. Security, Benefits
Vehicle Cost	-	-	8	8	- where applicable
Travel/Entert	-	-	26	32	
Service Costs	5	5	5	5	- telephone, etc.
Direct Costs (Budgeted)	60	74	131	174	
Space costs	6	6	6	6	- Rent, Power, Light, Heating
Mach & Equip	10	10	10	10	- Office furniture & Equip.
Finance Director	20	20	20	20	- Co-ord./Accounting/Training/Temps
RO HR	12	12	12	12	- Personnel admin., Reception
RO IT	15	15	15	15	- PCs, E-mail, Printers, Support
Overhead Costs	63	63	63	63	
Total Cost of FTE	123	137	194	237	
Cost / Hour	$64 Bf 1980	$71 Bf 2190	$101 Bf 3120	$123 Bf 3800	(assuming 100% productive time)

The cost model should show support activity costs separately from the activities to which they are reallocated, so that managers responsible for support activities can manage their resource levels in response to changes in customer demand at the front line, or to policy changes which influence the level of infrastructure or sustaining activity in the business.

Sustaining activities

Sustaining activities consume resources *now*, but deliver benefit in the *future*. By definition, they have little or no cause-and-effect relationship with current products, services and customers. It is possible to run an enterprise with no sustaining activity at all, but rarely on a permanent basis.

Examples of sustaining activity are research and development, systems development, market research, prospecting for new customers. (Note that prospecting for new customers is only a sustaining activity if it results in an increased customer base: customer 'churn' – or replacement of lost customers – is really driven by the reason for losing customers.)

Sustaining activity costs should *not* be attributed to current products and customers when measuring profitability or in support of pricing decisions. It is commercially unrealistic to expect current customers to pay for the results of research which do not yet exist and which they did not commission. Forcing the issue by apportioning such costs across current products or customers may well make them appear unprofitable. If as a result management withdrew from such products or customers the company would be worse off financially – *because the apportioned cost would not be avoidable as a consequence of that decision.*

Infrastructure activities

Infrastructure activities are necessary to stay in business. Their cost is completely independent of business volumes. Examples are the cost of the annual audit, the chairman's lunch, determining health and safety policy, and producing year-end statutory accounts.

Any attempt to allocate infrastructure costs to cost objects is pure apportionment: the concept of infrastructure cost drivers is meaningless.

In true activity based accounting for a self-supporting business, infrastructure activity costs (and sustaining activity costs in the long run) have to be covered by the margin between sales revenue and the costs of direct materials plus front-line and supporting activities.

The ABC model

Attributing the costs of activities on the basis of these differences provides a more rational understanding of how contribution is generated. This is illustrated in Figure 25.

Figure 25 ABC model

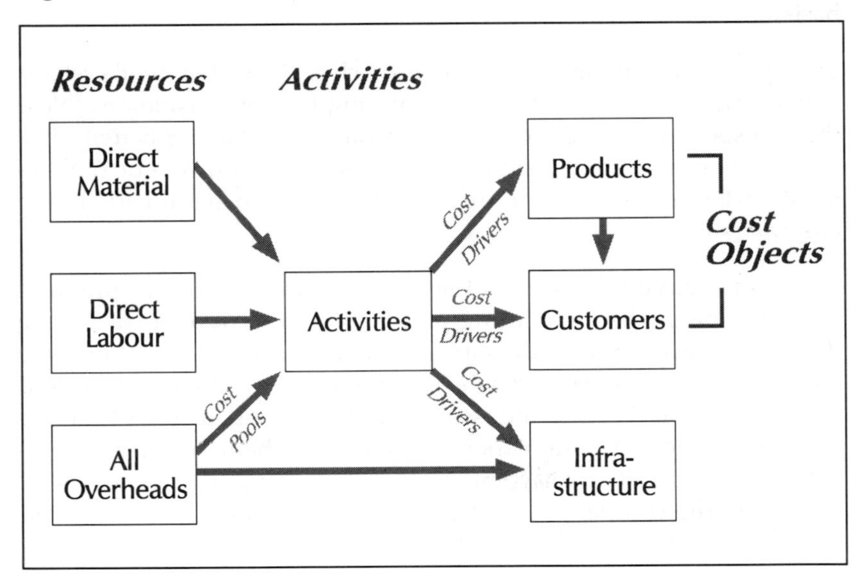

The important thing about this model is that it does not force non-product related costs into a *product* costing 'corset'. Instead, it recognises that there is a clear division between customer and product related costs, and that they should be analysed separately. It also makes a clear distinction between activity costs that have a strong causal relationship to products, services and customers (front-line activities), those that can only be related indirectly (support activities), and those that cannot be related to current outputs at all (sustaining and infrastructure activities). This important distinction allows for a clear separation between *attributable* and *apportioned* activities, and therefore allows a clear distinction between a marginal and full absorption approach to activity based costing. This clarity of understanding of cost behaviour is essential if management decision making is not to be distorted.

Allocation of costs to activities

Once activities are defined, regardless of their level of detail, the next step is to cost them. General ledger costs need to be translated into activity costs, as illustrated in Figure 26.

Figure 26 Translation of general ledger costs to activity costs

Expense Headings	General Ledger Costs (£k)
Staff Costs	243
N.I., Pension, etc.	54
Company Cars	18
Telephone	16
Stationery	3
Accomodation	41
I.T. Support	37
Staff Restaurant	4
	416

Activities	Activity Costs (£k)
Evaluate new suppliers	*25
Develop new components purchasing programmes	43
Negotiate with suppliers	*62
Process orders	138
Supplier intelligence	18
Resolve supplier problems	64
Departmental admin.	39
Staff training	27
	416

There are three bases on which these costs are usually allocated. They can be:

1 People costs are normally allocated to activities in proportion to the *time* they spend on different activities. People costs normally include

salaries and associated expenses, and other directly people related costs such as company cars, telephone, stationery, and general office equipment. Depending on the nature of the decisions to be supported by the resulting information, it may also be appropriate to include a share of staff occupancy costs.

2 Some costs are self-evidently *activity specific* – for example, contract delivery costs, or equipment dedicated to a specific task, such as a bank ATM.

3 Some costs are *cost object specific*: these often relate to bought-in goods and services, and should be allocated directly. Examples include subcontracted work specific to a particular customer (such as specialist artwork), the cost of advertising a particular product, and components bought for a particular product or customer.

Identifying cost drivers

Because conventional costing systems tend to allocate 'overhead' costs on the basis of volumes alone, they obscure the way they are *driven*. Cost drivers should form the basis for the costing system to reflect reality, and therefore provide its credibility with line management.

The following is a useful framework for facilitating the discussion of cost drivers in a consistent way in an organisation.

There are three generic types of cost driver:

1 volume cost drivers;

2 structural cost drivers;

3 change cost drivers.

The last two – structural and change drivers – are usually obscured from management by the inadequacies of conventional approaches to costing.

Volume cost drivers

Volume cost drivers measure the volume of output produced by an organisation. In a steel business it might be tonnes, in a brewery it might be gallons, in an insurance company it might be the value of premium income or claims paid, and in a bank it might include the total value of loans advanced. Whatever the context of the business it is intended to be a pure measure of volume generated. It may be supplemented by such measures as labour hours or machine hours. In essence, the greater the volume produced the greater the raw value added to the business.

Structural cost drivers

Structural cost drivers fragment the volume of a business and are often a major differentiator of profitability between competing organisations. They reflect the range of components, suppliers, raw materials, product variants, customers, orders, order lines, deliveries, and so forth, that a company has to manage. Such variety and complexity are major drivers of cost.

In conventional standard costing systems, for example, set-up activity is treated as part of the overhead, and is recovered into the product costs regardless of batch size. This distorts the accuracy of the product cost, thereby encouraging management to take on small orders in the belief that they are profitable, and to underestimate the profitability of larger orders. Providing visibility of the high costs implicit in small batch sizes spurs management to:

- reduce set-up costs;
- encourage customers to place larger orders;
- seek a premium for smaller batch sizes.

Failure to recognise these issues has led to many companies developing an 'overheads' problem, the root cause of which has been the inability of their costing systems to reflect anything more than volume alone. Once they have addressed the overheads problem through a cost-cutting exercise, they are then surprised to find that the problem recurs for no obvious reason.

> *In the early 1980s a well-known white goods manufacturer was concerned to reduce substantially the overall operating costs of its two manufacturing operations – one in the south east, the other in the north west. They had three options:*

1 concentrate all manufacture in the south;

2 concentrate all manufacture the north;

3 reduce operating costs on both sites.

The conventional internal management information indicated strongly that the southern factory had lower unit product costs. However, further investigation revealed that this plant manufactured only a limited range of products in high volumes, while the northern plant manufactured a large variety of much lower-volume products in small batches. Ironically, the northern production facilities were more modern and were ideally suited to high-volume manufacture, while the facilities in the south were better suited to low-volume manufacture.

Once the structural cost-drivers were identified for each site, the decision to concentrate manufacture in the north became clear. Implementation of this decision led to a significant improvement in profitability.

Change cost drivers

There are three different types of change cost driver. They are:

1 introduction cost drivers;

2 quality cost drivers;

3 'churn' cost drivers.

Introduction cost drivers

Increasing the number of parts that a company handles has many implications. For example, there will be an increase in the number of suppliers used, in the complexity of the stock management system, in levels of inventory, in the capability of manufacturing plant, in the training of manufacturing personnel, in the costs of quality and reliability assurance, in warranty costs, and in product and component testing. None of these increases would be reflected in the 'standard' cost of producing or purchasing a new component.

When designing new printed circuit boards, Hewlett Packard discovered that the cost of introducing a new component from a new supplier was up to five times greater than the cost of using an existing component.

To varying degrees the activities of research, design and development influence the future shape of the business. The costs of these activities are generally written off in the period in which they are incurred, even though the benefits may flow for several years. Decisions taken within these areas have a major impact on the future cost structure of the whole organisation and on product costs; costs which are generally hidden from management.

Introduction costs are hidden unless designers and their managers are reliably informed of the wider cost consequences of their design decisions, such as whether to design a new component or use an existing one.

The basic elements of the design cycle are well understood. However, the cost implications of the cycle are not. Figure 27 illustrates the problem.

Figure 27 The design cycle

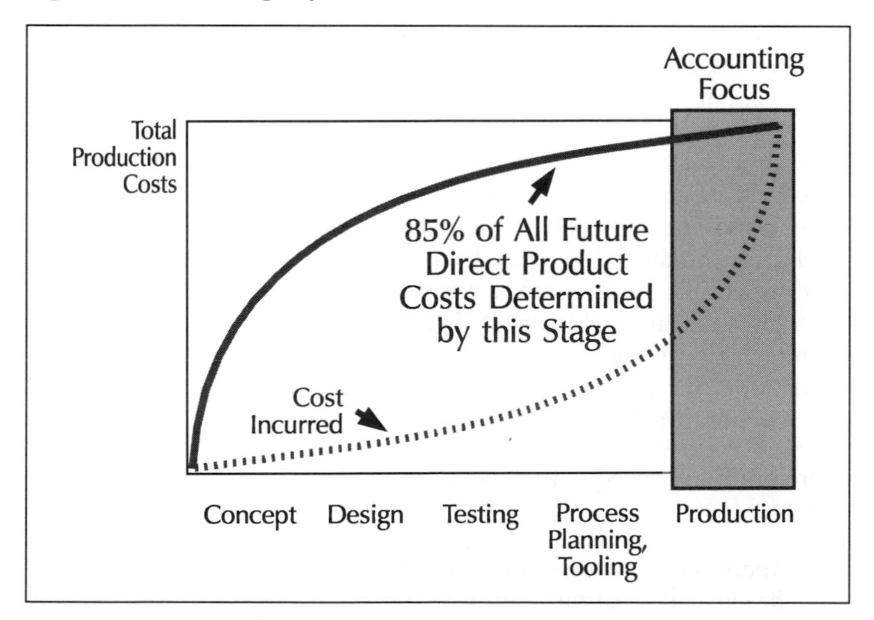

As the design and development process moves from concept to production, so the associated cash outflow increases according to the profile shown by the lower line. Conventionally, the finance function becomes most closely involved when cash outflow becomes significant – that is, towards the end of the cycle, when manufacturing plant is being installed, the workforce recruited and trained, pre-production stocks purchased, and the production process starts up.

The earlier stages incur relatively little expenditure: thinking is cheap. But the leverage of the early 'thinking' stages on the later cash-hungry stages of the development cycle is very high.

The profile of the upper line is therefore more significant. It illustrates the rate at which *future unit product costs* are determined by the design and development process. For example, in the design of a motor car, very early design decisions (size, power, transmission, saloon/hatchback) will determine a significant proportion of the future final unit cost. As a new product progresses through the design cycle, an increasing proportion of future costs become 'fixed', so that by the end of the testing phase some 85 per cent of future unit product costs are, to all intents and purposes, fixed for the life of the product. The only scope to modify these costs lies in relatively minor changes to product design and materials, or in improving the production process itself.

This reinforces the need to ensure that the original specification most closely meets customers' needs, and that the design is itself 'right first time', removing the need for unnecessary and expensive design or production modification. Establishing multi-disciplinary teams from the outset of the design process ensures a higher probability of achieving 'right first time'. This principle is of course not only applicable to manufacturing: it applies equally to product development in the service sector – for example, to the design of computer software, or the launch of a new life insurance product.

There are two consequences when such costs are not visible to management:

1 Companies often extend and diversify their product range too readily, because they seriously underestimate the costs of producing new products. This trend has been particularly evident in the financial services sector since deregulation

2 Companies make little attempt to rationalise their product ranges, because they fail to recognise the serious cost implications of a proliferation in parts and products.

Quality cost drivers

Quality costs arise in design and development because all component designs are subject to modification and refinement in the light of feedback from both customers and the manufacturing process itself. This is a valid 'quality cost'.

If a designer is unaware that a component already exists which has the necessary functionality, he or she will not only redesign the basic component but will also duplicate the quality cost of modification and refinement. A further consequence of redesigning what already exists is that there is less time left to produce the best design for what genuinely needs to be new. This 'reinvention of wheels' is one of the most common causes of high design and development costs, of extended product development cycles, and of excessive warranty costs.

Investing in processes that will make designers aware of what is already available internally and from existing external suppliers, and of the costs of these alternatives, will help to ensure that scarce skills, capabilities and time are devoted to activities that genuinely add value or differentiate the company and its products in the market place.

'Churn' cost drivers

Churn can be best described as a 'new-for-old' change. Many organisations experience significant amounts of 'churn' which is both an expensive drain on management time and disruptive to the business. An example of churn which affects many organisations is that of staff turnover. While dealing with normal levels of staff turnover is an integral part of business as usual, if the level of such turnover becomes abnormally high it can create considerable organisational strain.

There are both direct and indirect costs associated with this strain. The direct costs relate to advertising and recruitment, induction and training, and so forth. The indirect costs are more difficult to assess, since they relate to the cost of moving people down the learning curve in a business or department which is new to them.

Three case studies illustrate the importance of 'churn' cost drivers:

(A) *One of the smaller courier companies had experienced volume growth that regularly exceeded 25 per cent for many years. However, in one particular country over a four-year period, this revenue growth had been accompanied by rapidly deteriorating profitability. Excluding the effect of inflation, the cost per transaction had been growing by almost 20 per cent while the revenue per transaction had been static. Analysis showed that while the growth in unit operational costs were also relatively stable, the growth in the cost of the central overhead functions had been dramatic.*

A significant factor was the company's approach to career development. Most staff had been recruited as couriers and, as the company had grown, they had been promoted into supervisory positions in operational areas and then into the overhead functions. While a strong motivator, such career development resulted in frequent moves from one job to another, often in different departments. In one function the average job tenure of managers was less than 12 months.

The result was an organisation in a constant state of flux: managers had little opportunity to move down the learning curve before moving on. Firefighting was the norm, in order to maintain the company's high service standards – the antithesis of a 'learning organisation'.

A more measured approach to managing career moves created a stable basis for developing competences. Reducing the volume of management changes (the churn cost driver) led to a measurable reduction in diversionary time and cost.

(B) *A UK life assurance company, like all of its direct competitors, has had to face up to the tightening of its regulatory environment. This meant significant change for the sales force, from their systems of remuneration to their approach to the selling of pensions products. Staff turnover rose to 35 per cent, along with the cost of recruiting, training (and losing) salespeople.*

The cost of maintaining a sales force of a given size and capability is now a major component of the company's cost structure. Recognition of the cost implications of this churn has motivated management to review radically their employment policies and practices in order to minimise the rate of staff attrition.

(C) *A motoring organisation was experiencing membership churn in excess of 10 per cent a year. It had to recruit many thousands of new members a year, just to maintain existing levels.*

Until an ABCM study revealed the enormous cost of membership churn, management had regarded the rate as acceptable. While the organisation recognised that it could do little to influence the mortality of its members, the potential benefit of reducing churn caused it to focus decisively on membership retention and the factors that influence it.

Examples of cost drivers

There is no 'standard' set of cost drivers: each company will have its own set. The number of cost drivers required will also vary considerably, depending on the company's circumstances. In the earlier stages of development of an ABCM model it is important to keep it simple; the model can always be refined at a later date if necessary.

The first step is to ensure that the activities within each department have been defined to a level of detail such that changes in the level of an activity, or group of activities, can reasonably be said to be related to one, and only one, cost driving factor.

Figure 28 shows examples of different types of cost driver.

Figure 28 Examples of cost drivers

Volume drivers	Structural drivers	Change drivers
Weight	Customers	*Introduction drivers*
Volume	Suppliers	New products
Value	Parts	Product changes
Materials	Products	New components
Labour content	Order lines	Prototypes
Machine hours	Works orders	New suppliers
	Batches	New customers
	Set-ups	
	Time-critical orders	*Quality drivers*
	Special orders	Derivative designs
	Late orders	Customer complaints
		Capability modifications
		Functional modifications
		Churn drivers
		Staff turnover
		Stock turnover
		Customer turnover
		Staff rotation
		Product supersession

Product-related overhead activities

In an ABC model, product costs are built from the following categories of cost:

- direct material;
- direct labour;
- product-related overheads that are *volume*-dependent;
- product-related overheads that are driven by *structural* and *change* cost drivers.

Figure 29 illustrates the result.

Figure 29 ABC Product costs

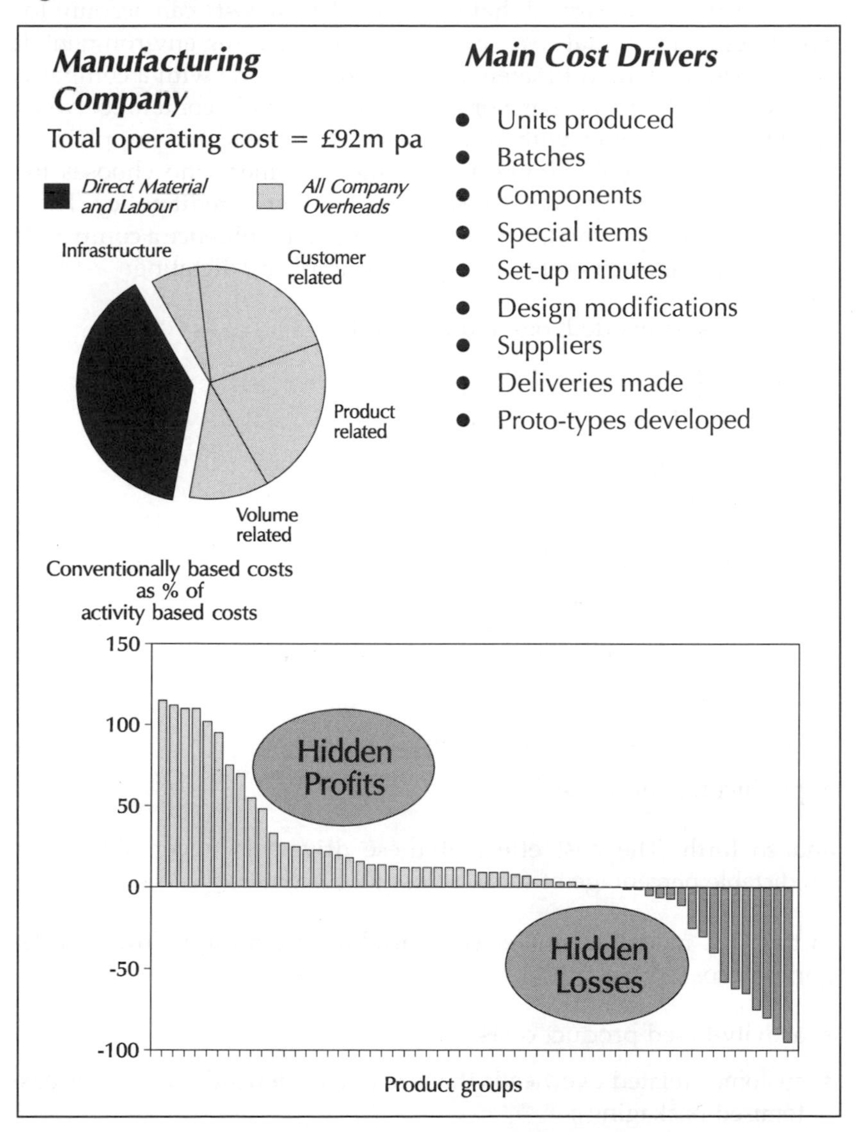

Customer-related overhead activities

We have already observed that customer-driven costs can account for over 50 per cent of total costs, even in a manufacturing environment. It is the customer who ultimately chooses how to trade with a company: for example, there is a major difference in work content between supplying a customer with 10 batches of 100 items, and supplying a single batch of 1,000. Similarly, it is the customer who chooses the number of debtor days, regardless of the supplier's credit policy. There are many different ways in which a customer can influence a company's costs and therefore its profitability, for example by dictating:

- discounts demanded, on- and off-invoice;
- order size;
- order and delivery frequency;
- packaging requirements;
- packing requirements;
- customised design modifications;
- testing and certification needs;
- stringency of quality needs;
- order frequency;
- late modifications to requirement;
- product mix purchased;

and so forth. The cost effect of these drivers is never a fixed or predictable percentage of sales, across all customers.

In the ABC model, customer costs are built from the following categories of cost:

- activity-based product costs;
- customer-related overheads that are *volume*-dependent (such as customised packaging);
- customer-related overheads that are driven by *structural* and *change* cost drivers.

Infrastructure and sustaining activities

As we discussed earlier, infrastructure and sustaining activity costs are those whose cost drivers are *not* related to current products, services or customers. They are therefore not avoidable in the short to medium term. They should be excluded from any ABC analysis whose purpose is to make product portfolio and make-or-buy decisions, simply because the cause – and – effect relationship is weak over this timescale and they cannot be 'avoided' as a consequence of related decisions.

However, if the need is to develop a 'full' product or customer cost, say for pricing and margin-management purposes, then activity analysis will provide a better basis for apportioning the costs which are not avoidable in this timescale.

Clearly, the more strategic the nature of the decisions required, the longer the time-frame and therefore, the greater the proportion of the overhead costs that can be regarded as 'decision-variable' before the contribution to remaining fixed costs and profit is defined.

The advantage of activity based over conventional approaches to costing

The main difference between conventional and ABC approaches is the proportion of overhead costs whose 'behaviour' is understood. This is illustrated in Figure 30.

Figure 30 ABC product costs

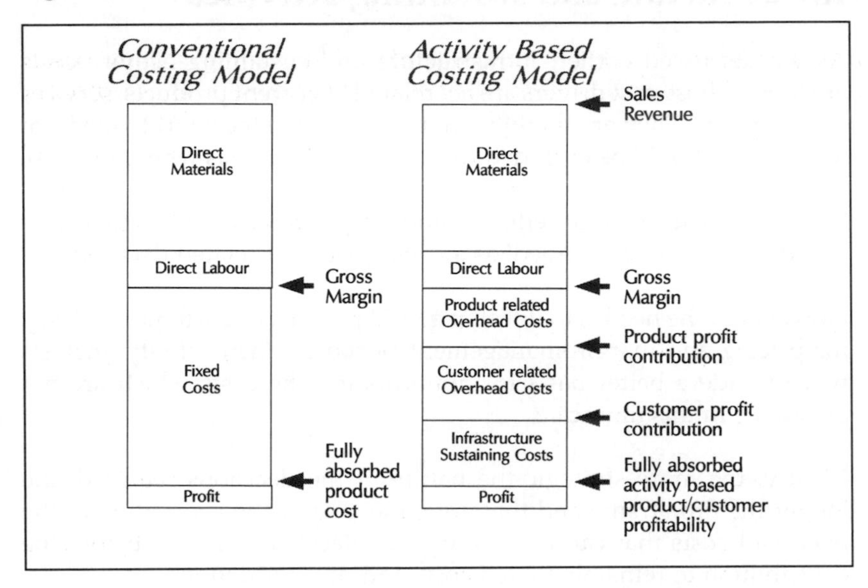

Because ABC properly recognises product-driven overhead activity costs, these can legitimately be regarded as marginal, and can therefore be included in the calculation of *product contribution*. Similarly, by adding customer-driven overhead costs, it is possible to define a marginal *customer contribution*.

It is therefore possible to understand the behaviour of a far higher proportion of total costs than with conventional costing methods. The proportion of total costs that has to be 'absorbed' (the sustaining and infrastructure activity costs) is therefore much lower, so that their distorting effect, while not eliminated, is much reduced.

Insights through analysis

Developing an ABC model is seldom straightforward, and credibility with the management that will use the information is critical. Presenting management with a raw activity database can be profoundly unexciting to them, unless it can be analysed in such a way as to reveal new insights into the nature of their business.

A fast-moving consumer goods manufacturer produces a relatively narrow range of base product, which is then finished and packaged into a very wide range of finished products and sold to a wide variety of customers, both in the UK and overseas. To manufacture the base product successfully requires a very carefully controlled manufacturing process in which even the smallest of errors can cause a whole batch to be scrapped.

As a consequence the company has always been strongly aware of the need for close adherence to strict quality control standards and procedures. This led them to be one of the earlier proponents of total quality as a management and working philosophy for the organisation.

Increasing pressure on margins caused them to initiate an ABC project to understand better the relative profitability of both products and customers. The approach was sophisticated because from the outset, management were intent on using the results to influence their decision making; they therefore needed a high degree of credibility.

The project team analysed the cost of front-line, support, sustaining and infrastructure activities. At the outset of the exercise, management were asked to give their expectation of the result – shown in the left-hand pie chart in Figure 31.

Figure 31 FMCG manufacturer – breakdown of overhead costs by type of activity

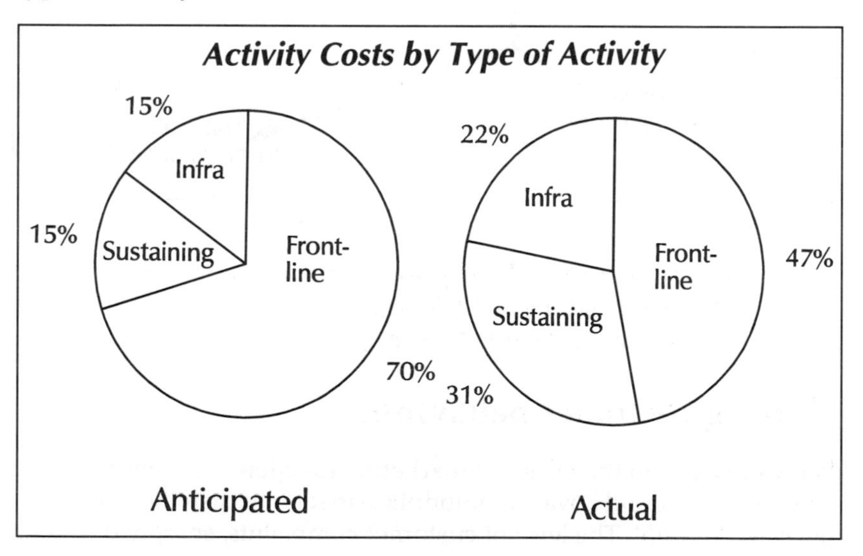

They were surprised by the actual profile that emerged. Supporting Total Quality was classified as sustaining activity, which turned out to cost twice what they expected.

The surprise was compounded when they examined the analysis of activity costs by type of cost driver, shown in Figure 32. Commercial management had believed it to be relatively inexpensive to introduce new product variants: the conventional costing system did not account for the extent to which product range complexity influenced attributable costs.

Figure 32 FMCG manufacturer – breakdown of overhead costs by type of cost driver

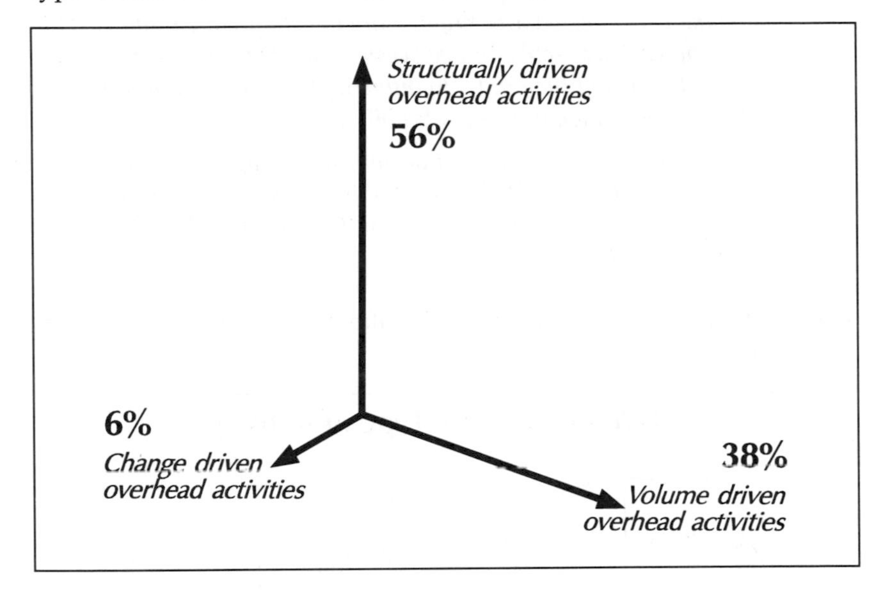

As a consequence, management placed greater emphasis on the delivery of benefits from its quality and re-engineering initiatives, and initiated a strategic review of the product range.

Costing customer behaviour

Some time ago, in the sales and marketing function of a manufacturing company, we found it was commonplace to refer to customers humour- [illegible]

sales and a redundancy programme rather took the edge off the joke. Customers buy products and services. No customers – no business.

Although conventional costing systems almost always provide inadequate product costs, they do at least recognise that products are different. So are customers. No two customers have the same needs, or the same expectations of service. Different customers place different demands for service. Some have greater power to demand higher levels of service and lower prices than others – as suppliers to grocery multiples will testify.

> *A drinks company was convinced that product complexity was the main cause of high manufacturing, distribution and overhead costs. Within manufacturing, this was true – they discovered significant costs associated with changeovers and inventory management. A strategic review eliminated a category of products, which reduced product complexity by a quarter. But overhead costs remained obstinately stable.*
>
> *Analysis of overhead activities by cost driver showed that more than three times as much cost in the organisation was driven by customer complexity than by product complexity. Most of this customer-driven cost was in commercial, distribution and accounting functions.*

Cost driver variability

In recent years, there has been some spirited debate between academics on the relationship between activities and cost drivers. The sceptics argued that the relationship was too simplistic, the protagonists that it was better than not attempting to make the connection at all. There is some truth in the sceptics' position, if ABC does not address the issue of variability within a cost driver.

The relationship between an activity and its cost driver is central to activity-based *costing*. It allows the calculation of the cost per unit cost driver, which then becomes the basis for costing the cost objects according to the volumes of the cost drivers which they consume.

Implicit in the definition of the cost per unit cost driver, such as the cost per purchase order processed, is the notion that each occurrence of the event, or purchase order in this case, costs exactly the same – illustrated in the first distribution diagram in Figure 33. This is clearly a simplification of the real world: the cause-and-effect relationship between an activity and its cost driver seldom exhibits such precision.

Common sense tells us that some sales orders take longer to process than others. An analysis of the time spent on a valid sample of purchase orders would usually produce the normal distribution illustrated by the second diagram in Figure 33.

Figure 33 Distribution of costs per unit cost driver

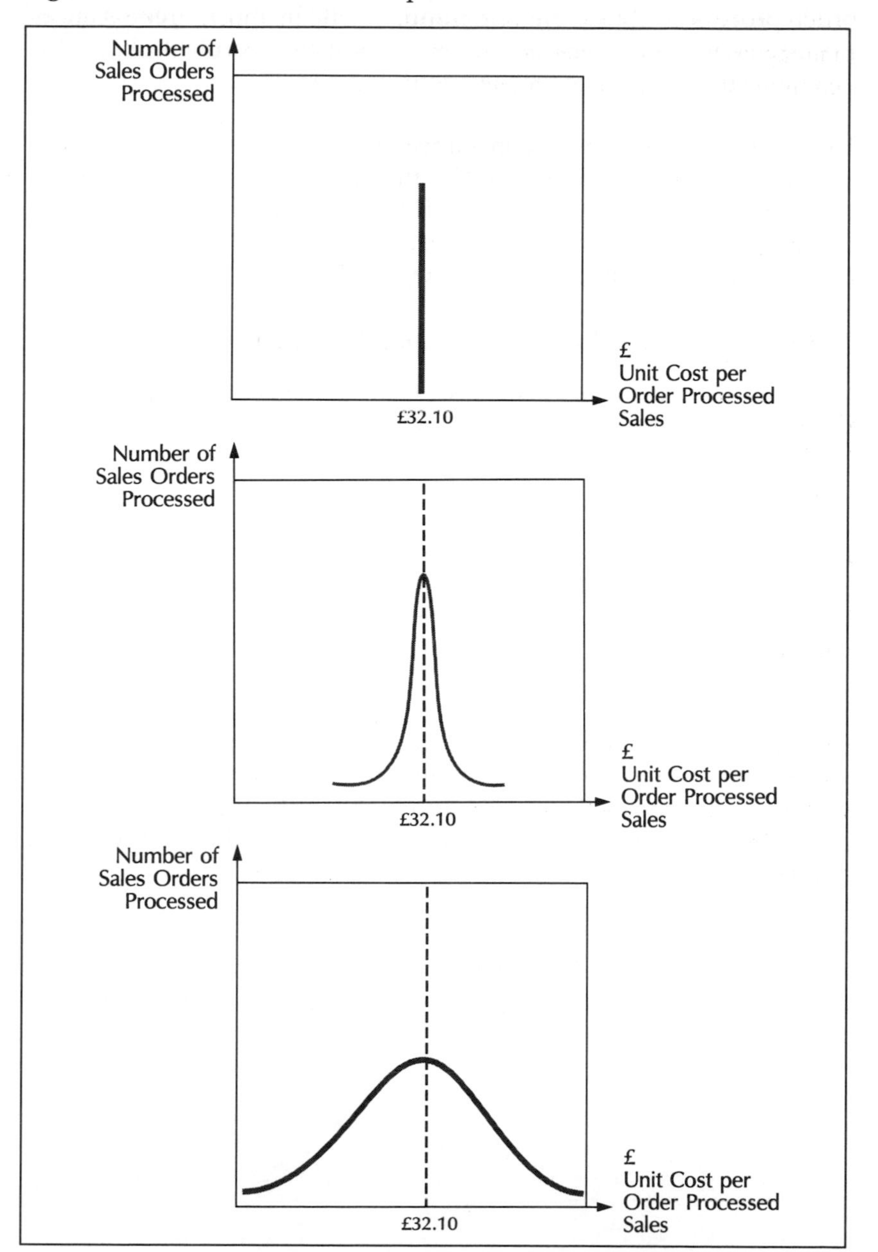

We can interpret this distribution as meaning that the cost per sales order processed is £32, plus or minus a bit. In most circumstances management would regard this as a perfectly acceptable basis for commercial and resource management decisions.

However, there may be circumstances in which the sample demonstrates wide variability illustrated by the third diagram in Figure 33, to the point where credibility is lost. Dealing with this involves either defining separate activities and cost drivers for different types of purchasing activity, or grading or weighting the cost driver.

Reflecting variability of customer behaviour

While no two customers behave in exactly the same way, staff will usually have a very clear view of which customers are time-consuming to deal with, and which are not. It is therefore possible to grade customer behaviour.

In one organisation, the primary salesforce activity was *visiting customers*, for which the cost driver was number of *customer visits*. The average time spent with each customer was 60 minutes. However, actual times varied between 20 minutes and two hours.

The *grading framework* illustrated in Figure 34 was developed and circulated to each member of the salesforce, inviting them to assess which grade best described the behaviour of each of their customers. It was then extended by the distribution of the visit – the cost driver. The resulting hash total became the basis for attributing the activity cost of *visiting customers*.

The activity cost of *visiting customers* thereby became customer specific, reflecting both the required frequency of visit, and the degree to which different customers are demanding of salespeople's time during each visit.

Figure 34 Cost driver grading

Customer	Av. Customer Grade/Visit	x	Frequency of Visit/Yr.	=	Weighting of Customer Effort	Customer Driven Cost
A	3		12		36	26,400
B	1		4		4	2,933
C	1		8		8	5,867
D	2		4		8	5,867
E	5		6		30	22,000
F	2		2		4	2,933
					90	66,000

Allocated to customer on basis of weighting

Total cost of key account salesman

The same kind of variability can apply to other customer-driven activities, such as distribution:

> *A UK distribution company recognised that the number of deliveries was the main driver for its fleet of vehicles and drivers. Customer deliveries took an average of five minutes, but vehicle drivers knew that some took over an hour. Analysis showed that deliveries to over 50 per cent of customers had been over-costed by more than 100 per cent, while the actual cost per delivery to 2 per cent of customers was 12 times the cost that had been previously calculated.*

Reflecting variability in product behaviour

A similar approach can be used to deal with variability in product cost drivers. For example, the number of set-ups may be inadequate to describe the variability in set-up times, which may be driven by the nature of the product or component to be made, or, more problematically, by the *sequence* of set-ups. The set-up time for a changeover from black paint to white paint is much longer than for a changeover from white paint to black paint. In some cases, set-up sequence may even be driven more by the nature of customer demand than by the products.

The activity cost of *machine setting* can therefore be made component- or product-specific, reflecting both the required frequency of set-up, and the degree of difficulty associated with each different type of set-up.

When to reflect customer or product cost driver variability

The need to reflect cost driver variability depends on the materiality of activity cost, and the degree of variability. The obvious benefit is that the ABC model more closely reflects reality, generating a higher degree of credibility for the results, and therefore ownership among those who must use them.

Where the cost effect of customer and product behaviour is assessed in a number of different departments, the ABC model both quantifies and integrates the effect to give a powerful picture of the overall impact of a product or a customer, often for the first time. Once customer and product behaviour is understood in this way, it can be influenced by management action. We discuss this issue further in the next chapter.

Summary

Successful development of an ABCM cost model depends on clear identification of the purposes for which it is to be used. The required *level of detail of activity data* depends on whether the model is to be used for commercial decision-making (such as product and customer costing and profitability) and resource management decisions, or for improvement purposes.

There are four distinct *categories of activity* – front-line, supporting, sustaining or infrastructure, which have different degrees of cause-and-effect relationship with *cost objects* (products and services, customers, sales channels, and so forth). The relationship is determined by *cost drivers*

Three *types of cost driver* exist – volume cost drivers, which measure output; structural cost drivers, which measure complexity; and change cost drivers.

Costing *variability in customer and product behaviour* is often an important factor in ensuring credibility for the model.

CHAPTER 6

ABCM to support profitability analysis and commercial management

ABC is useless – unless you do something with it.

Professor Robert Kaplan
Harvard Business School

In Chapter 3 we discussed positioning and capability, and a framework for ABCM that distinguishes between different types of initiative which activity based techniques can support. In this chapter we concentrate on the *management* part of the ABCM framework, and in particular the predominantly external emphasis on profitability analysis and commercial decision support. It is this element of ABCM that addresses positioning.

Activity based information in support of commercial decision making derives from the activity based *costing* (ABC) techniques. These include both activity based product, service and customer costing, and contribution analysis. It is not about efficiency and effectiveness. This we discuss in the next chapter.

The purpose of activity based costs

If the interest in activity based product costing is merely to develop more accurate inventory valuation figures for the purpose of SSAP 9, the effort is probably unwarranted, since the existing basis is likely to be already acceptable to the auditors. However, if the accuracy of those costs is likely materially to affect the commercial decisions of the company, then it is highly appropriate.

In practice, companies set prices by a combination of cost-plus and market-led considerations. The importance of accurate product costing lies in the nature of decisions that are made in relation to the resulting margins. If, as a consequence of poor product costs, the margin is understated, there is likely to be little interest either in investing in the product, or in allocating to it operating resources such as sales and marketing. On the other hand, if margin is overstated, such resources *will* be devoted to it. This will result in a consistently inadequate return, with little understanding of why performance is so hard to improve, despite goodwill and hard work. It may also create an 'overheads problem'.

The proportion of costs that management can influence *in the short-term* is diminishing–because an increasing proportion is the result of investments in automation, systems, and so forth. Furthermore, labour costs are not actually 'variable' in the sense that they can be influenced in the short term – except labour that is paid solely on a *genuine* piecework basis. Therefore, costing of products and customers is primarily about two issues:

1 short-term deployment of resources and utilisation of capacity;

2 medium- to long-term decision making.

The first highlights the increasing importance of building as much flexibility as possible into the company's operations, especially in its workforce, for example through multi-skilling and flexible manufacturing facilities. The second recognises that *in the short term* relatively few costs can be varied by management. ABC supports three main areas of commercial decision-support:

1 portfolio decisions;

2 pricing and margin management decisions;

3 customer access and micro-marketing decisions.

Portfolio decisions

These directly affect the range of products a company wishes to produce, or the types of customers it wishes to trade with. Equally, make/buy and subcontract decisions also fall in this category.

The notions of 'traceability' and 'avoidability' of costs are central to such decisions. These require a direct causal relationship between activity and cost object, usually expressed in terms of a cost driver. The resources which these activities consume must therefore be capable of either being removed from the company, or being re-allocated to other productive activities. If a cost driver does not reasonably reflect such a causal relationship, management cannot respond positively to the implementation implications for resources of this type of decision. Costs which can only be *apportioned* should normally therefore be excluded for the purposes of such portfolio decisions.

Pricing and margin management decisions

Where management wish to draw comfort from knowing the fully absorbed cost of production of a product or provision of a service to a customer, cost drivers *can* be used as a basis for apportioning those costs for which there is no causal relationship between activity and object. This will merely produce a more refined fully absorbed cost. Infrastructure costs at different organisational levels, such as space costs, are likely to be treated in this way. Although more refined, such costs will still suffer from all the problems associated with apportionment of costs.

Information shown in this way does have some value as an attention-directing device, focusing management effort on ensuring that even those resources that can demonstrate no direct causal relationship with either product or customer in the short to medium term are adding value to the organisation.

The different approaches of marginal and full absorption costing are just as relevant in an activity based environment as they are in a conventional environment.

Accurate product costing provides invaluable support to pricing decisions, particularly when margins are tight.

> *The British Printing Industry Federation (BPIF) has long given guidance to its members, many of them small and medium-sized companies, on the basis that they should use to cost their estimates for new jobs. This is of particular importance as virtually all printing jobs are different and each requires a separate quotation. The basis of this advice was a conventional,*

full absorption approach to costing, where large parts of the overhead costs are absorbed on machine hours.

A medium-sized printer equipped to meet a wide range of customer requirements, from low-cost football programmes to high quality published company accounts found the order book full of many small orders, while the success rate in attracting large orders was limited. Management were concerned that their estimating system was not sufficiently reflecting the true cost of complexity in their business.

As a consequence they established an alternative, activity-based estimate of the likely cost of each job they tendered for. It indicated that some small jobs were being regularly under-estimated by between 50 and 60 per cent of the corresponding activity-based cost; it was hardly surprising that they were having such success, albeit unwelcome, in attracting small orders. By contrast the conventional approach was over-costing the larger jobs by some 30 per cent, most of which had been lost to competitors. Further analysis revealed that, had they trimmed the estimates of their quotations for the larger jobs by 10 per cent, their success rate would have been a lot higher, while still making a healthy positive contribution.

Within three months the average job size had risen from £1,700 to over £3,000, and profitability had increased dramatically.

Customer access and micro-marketing decisions

Most organisations aspire to understand profit contribution by product, channel and customer. However, companies that serve a market consisting of many, geographically diverse, customers such as the financial services and retail sectors, find it harder to generate actionable commercial decisions at the level of the individual customer, even if they could identify profitability at that level.

Organisations decide where to locate the physical access points (outlets) through which individual customers can transact business with it. However, all other things being equal, and often even when they are not, the customer will then choose to purchase on the basis of the convenience of the access point. Hence the adage that in retailing, the three most important factors are location, location and location. *Therefore understanding the profit contribution derived from the area served by a particular customer access point, and what influences that at a micro, customer-level, becomes critical to the decision of where to locate outlets for maximum commercial advantage.*

Developing an understanding of the external processes of customer choice at the small geographical level enables an organisation to manipulate the location of access points in such a way as to increase market share in any given locality. This is known as micromarketing. It seeks to answer a question which process re-engineering often fails to address: 'if market share reflects competitive advantage, and this is based on price and customer service, why is it that market share varies so much between different locations within the same region?'

Understanding customer service needs

The reason for understanding the profitability of individual or groups of customers or products is not to act as a substitute for sound commercial and strategic judgement; rather it is to inform it better. It is equally important to have a proper appreciation of the competitive importance of customers' service needs, *and* the extent and circumstances under which customers might be prepared to modify their service requirements.

All management teams believe that they have a sound understanding of their customers' service needs. However, our experience of customer needs surveys frequently shows differences between what the customers want and what management think they want.

> *An office equipment supplier decided to put its understanding of its customers' service needs to the test. They developed a list of some forty customer service factors and asked customers to identify those they considered to be most influential on their buying decision. They then asked the customers to rate their performance against those factors compared with the competition. The results are shown in Figure 35.*

All too often organisations do best what is easiest, rather than what is most important to the customer. It is very easy for management to make such poorly informed decisions, and for their staff to work extremely hard on things which the customer does not really care about. Under these circumstances the only ones to benefit are the competitors who have understood.

ure 35 Office equipment supplier – customer needs survey

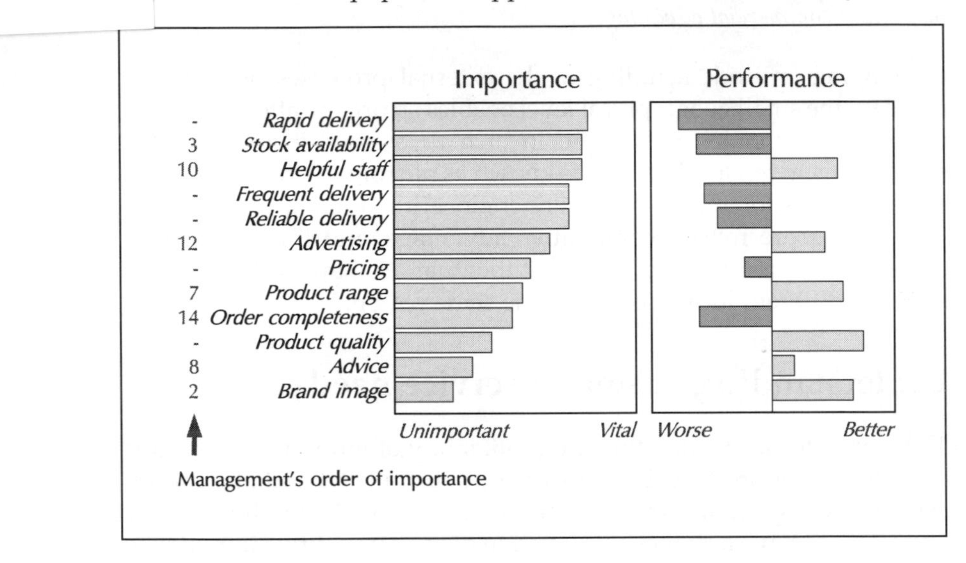

Analysis of activity based product and customer profitability

Developing an understanding of product and customer costs through activity based approaches has a number of benefits, not least the greater understanding of cost/activity relationships and cost driver accountability engendered in management and staff.

However, the greatest value emerges when these costs are set against the sales revenues to which they relate, to identify product or customer contribution. By developing a clear understanding of which products and customers contribute strongly to the bottom-line, as opposed to those which erode it, management can focus scarce resources to greatest advantage. After all, hard work brings no guarantee of success – merely of fatigue.

Because most organisations have a fairly wide range of products and customers, knowing the profit contribution of each one, while important in itself, is insufficient in helping to frame or modify commercial policies or strategy. To achieve this, and to focus management attention on action, it is important to be able to analyse such data. The following techniques are particularly helpful, whether they are applied to product or customer profitability analysis, by making *patterns* visible in the way that numbers alone do not. To avoid repetition we have focused on customer profitability, but the lessons hold equally true for product profitability.

Cumulative customer contribution analysis (CCCA)

This technique highlights how major resources (and assets) frequently stand behind those customers that generate only marginal or negative contributions. It illustrates graphically the extent of profit erosion by customers with servicing costs that exceed the margins which they generate. Figure 36 shows a typical result of such analysis.

Figure 36 Cumulative customer profitability analysis

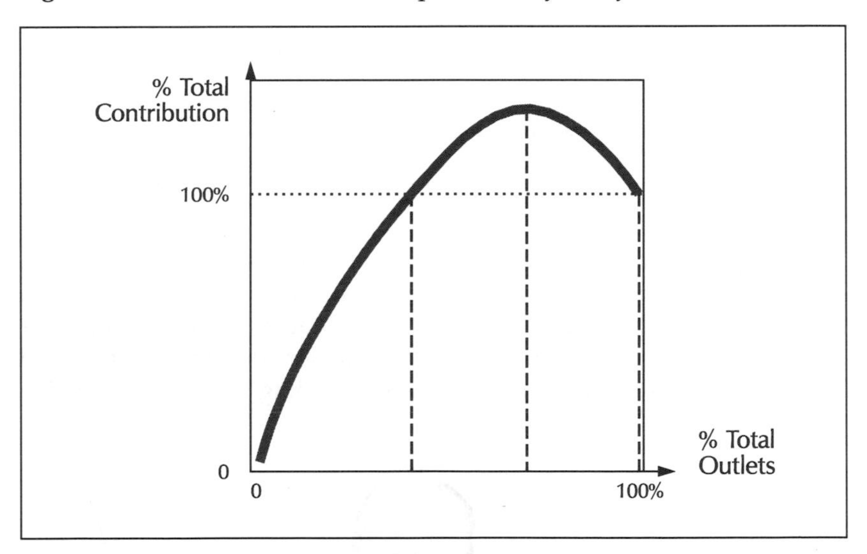

These 'hook diagrams' frequently identify examples of profit erosion to the extent of 20 to 40 per cent of the profit which has already been generated, and there are documented examples as high as 60 per cent.

Decision grid analysis (DGA)

This technique plots each account on a graph of profitability against volumes of business, as illustrated in Figure 37.

Figure 37 Decision grid analysis

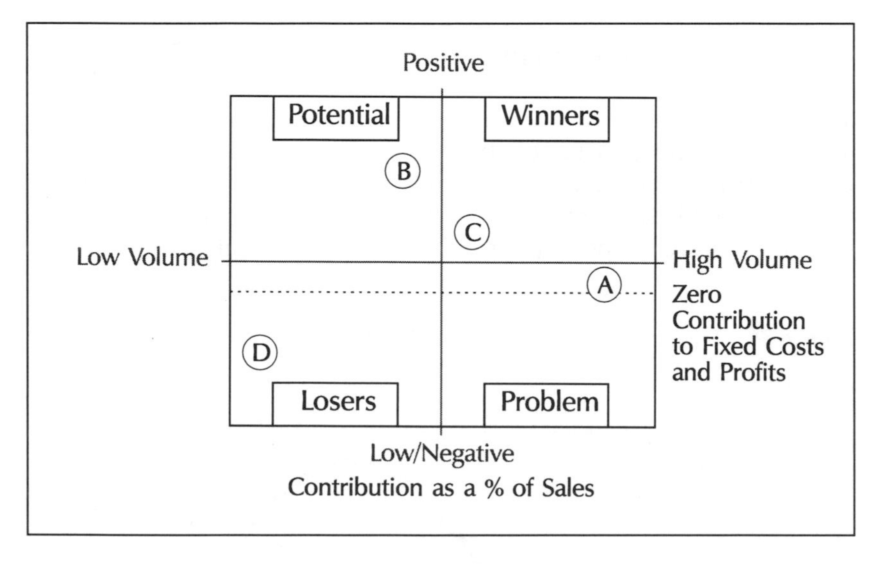

It highlights all customer accounts against one of four categories, each of which will require a different commercial response. It is also the first step in defining the characteristics of a profitable or unprofitable customer, so providing the company with a greater ability to identify, and then focus resources on developing and defending genuinely attractive accounts.

Mix analysis

The thinking which underpins decision grid analysis can also be used to develop a powerful understanding of how the *mix of product* purchased by a particular customer contributes to their overall profitability. In particular, this form of analysis frequently highlights anomalies in pricing and discount structures.

A manufacturer of commercial film recognised that its largest customer in the UK was only just generating a positive contribution, and wished to understand the reasons. They analysed the customer's contribution by product, with the result shown in Figure 38.

Figure 38 Customer product contribution analysis

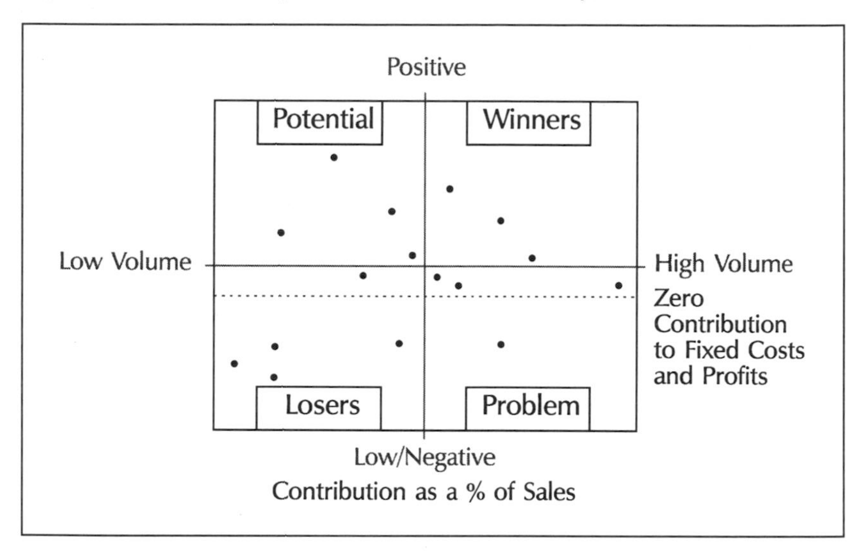

The analysis revealed that while many products made an attractive return there were many more which were either low volume and/or negative contributors. With this information available it was then possible for the company to initiate a constructive win-win discussion with the customer about the nature of the trading relationship between them, based on the costs driven by that relationship.

Vertical profitability analysis

Many large organisations are vertically integrated to some extent. Each division or operating company acts as a profit centre, with internal transfer pricing to enable measurement of business unit profitability. Pricing based on inaccurate costing systems, combined with conflicting objectives can led to serious distortions.

A European steel manufacturer operated on a truly international basis, often with different stages in the manufacturing process taking place in different countries. For example, steel slab produced in a melting shop in the UK could be hot rolled in Germany and cold rolled in Belgium before being sold through the UK selling company. At each point of exchange in the manufacturing process a transfer price would be applied, and each manufacturing site's performance assessed on the basis of its 'profitability'.

Problems showed most strongly in the selling companies, who were the victims of conflicting imperatives: they were required to maximise throughput because of the capital intensive nature of the steel business, but also to maximise the profitability of sales.

The root of the problem lay in the lack of visibility of what part of the total margin was taken at which stage of the manufacturing process. To create this visibility, activity and cost driver analyses were undertaken at each stage of the manufacturing process, so that the way costs were driven through the entire process cost chain, from slab to end customer, was understood. It was then feasible to strip out the internal, inter-site transfer prices and develop an end-to-end view of profitability by both product and customer.

This revealed that the apparent profitability of some products and customers was significantly at variance with reality, and led to a radical overhaul of how product and customer profitability were assessed, how plant performance was reported, and how products were priced. While implementation required some political effort by senior management – some long-standing parochial sacred cows were slaughtered in the process – the effect was a significant improvement in the company's ability to compete internationally and profitably.

Action out of analysis

Such analyses are of course of no value unless they lead to action. In the case of customer profitability, the four main ways of achieving this are:

1 productivity improvements;

2 customer engineering;

3 commercial strategy;

4 competitor modelling.

Productivity improvements

Before embarking on an activity based costing exercise, it is essential to make sure that the company's overall operations are as cost effective as possible. Failure to do this may cause the cost of current inefficiencies to be attributed to products or customers, thereby distorting the outcome.

Many seem to achieve a competitive level of productivity by undertaking reviews of technology, resource utilisation, performance and planning in each function. But, although yielding some benefits, such reviews are generally limited in their results because they are function based; they cannot take account of inefficiencies within the web of interfunctional relationships on which every company depends for its day-to-day operations.

The quickest, most effective way of fully understanding all overhead activities and what drives them – is to undertake a thorough review of overhead effectiveness. The key elements of such a review are described in Chapter 7.

Customer engineering

Customer engineering asks critical questions and compares and evaluates answers: its purpose is to enhance the company's profitability to an acceptable level in respect of each customer. For example:

- What is the maximum discount allowable before a customer ceases to be profitable?
- What will be the impact of distributing to major customers via their national distribution centres rather than through our own network?
- How will EDI affect cost structure?
- What is the implication of serving smaller customers through third-party wholesalers?
- Which are the least profitable customers and how can their profitability be most easily improved?

- How can the sales force be directed towards more profitable new customers, rather than chasing volume alone?
- How can we best protect our most profitable customers?

If customer engineering is to be successful, it is important:

- that managers recognise that customer expectations of service, in all its forms, can be managed;
- that there is a commitment to modify the internal cost structure to reflect any changes resulting from customer engineering;
- that customer engineering decisions are carefully planned and the results monitored;
- that top management commitment exists, especially in view of the cross-functional nature of the effect of some decisions.

Customer engineering is the equivalent of exchanging a shotgun for a sniper's rifle in support of commercial decision making. It is no substitute for commercial judgement, but it does provide a sounder basis for making decisions.

Commercial strategy

A clear view of customer profitability is essential for evaluating and developing a sound commercial strategy; it is the only way of linking the company's external trading relationship at customer level to its internal cost structure. This is not an end in itself but a base for developing a more credible and focused strategy. It complements the company's understanding of the market, the players within it and its own competitive positioning.

Useful techniques include:

Outlier fixing

This seeks to identify the normal pattern of contribution behaviour, in order to isolate products or customers whose performance varies significantly from this norm. By this means both extraordinary performance and problems can be recognised, and lessons learnt.

'Hook' curves

The 'hook', or cumulative contribution curves described earlier in this chapter can be manipulated on a 'what if' basis to model the consequences of changes in pricing and discount strategies. Two alternative pricing strategies are illustrated in Figure 39.

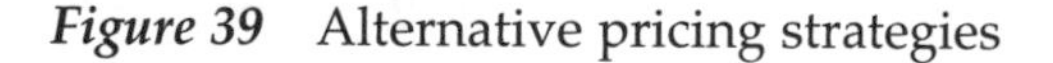

Figure 39 Alternative pricing strategies

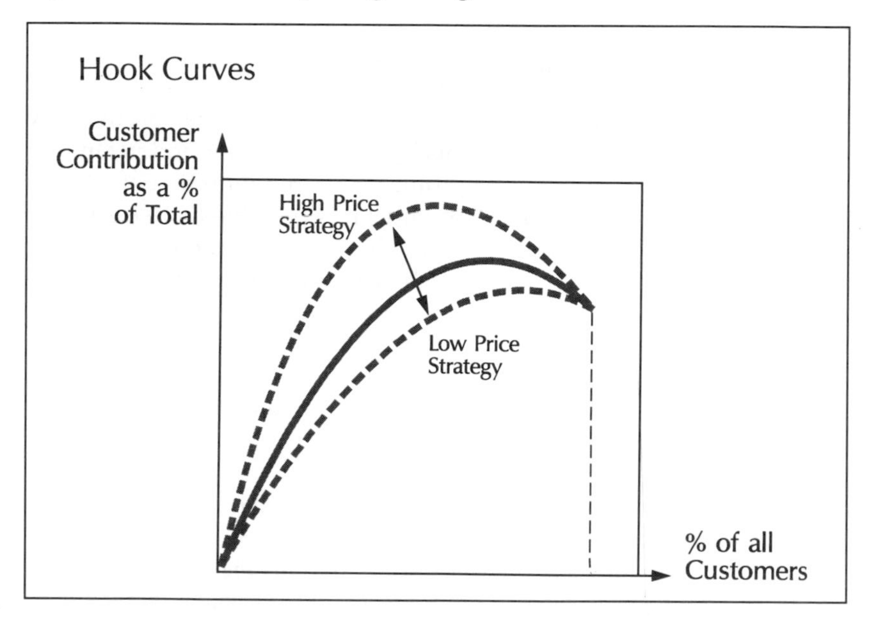

For example, if a premium pricing strategy were introduced, the 'hook' curve would rise more steeply, reflecting the effect of those customers who were prepared to accept the higher prices. However, it is equally likely that the larger customers would insist on correspondingly larger discounts in order to offset the price rises. The effect may or may not be a rise in overall contribution, but it would almost certainly be a higher risk commercial strategy, since it would tend to create a bigger price umbrella which might encourage lower-price competitors to enter the marketplace.

By contrast, if a lower pricing policy were pursued, the rate at which contribution might be accrued from the customer base might be lower, but the degree of subsequent erosion might also be correspondingly less. This approach to pricing would also make it much more difficult for a potential competitor to 'cherry-pick' the best accounts.

The ability to carry out such strategic and tactical 'what if' exercises with meaningful product and customer revenue and contribution data can make a major impact on the development of innovative commercial policies.

Competitor modelling

Competitor modelling is a natural extension of customer profitability analysis. The company achieves this by establishing an understanding of its own customer profitability profile compared with that of a target competitor. By evaluating the differences it is possible to assess which customers, segments and activities of the target competitor are most vulnerable to competitive action. Such evaluation is a valuable supplement to both market intelligence and intuitive feel for the right decision.

The following case study demonstrates the potential for using these techniques to bring about profitable change.

> *A wholesaler and distributor of a mature product range to the retail sector had grown, through extensive acquisition and organic growth, from a struggling medium-sized regional player into the market leader. It provided a nationwide delivery service to 18,000 customers through more than 60 warehouses.*
>
> *Management recognised that, given the maturity of the market, further profit growth could only come through better cost management.*
>
> *The company operated a complex volume-related discount and incentive structure and believed it to be effective in ensuring that all customers, whether large or small, were sources of profitable business. However, this view was intuitive. No evidence of customer profitability was available other than at gross margin level (net of trade discount).*
>
> *The warehouse and distribution network was a major element of operating costs and was substantially fixed in the short to medium term. The*

company therefore planned to rationalise and redesign the network to gain economies of scale and to take advantage of improvements in the trunk road and motorway network.

It first undertook a customer service needs survey. The most important finding was that a delivery service that was predictable and reliable was significantly more important to customers than one that was fast. This led to a policy shift in the delivery pattern and allowed distribution and sales managers to plan for a much more cost-effective use of sales and delivery resources.

Once the activity costs of servicing customers had been set against the gross margin generated at the level of individual customer outlets, it was possible to draw a cumulative outlet contribution analysis – a hook curve.

The chart revealed two surprises:

- *the cumulative contribution of the least profitable 60 per cent of customers was zero;*
- *the cost of serving each of the least profitable 28 per cent of customers was significantly greater than the gross margin they generated.*

An even more worrying revelation was that the largest customer, a major company representing some 20 per cent of total turnover, was generating a large negative contribution. Management sought to improve this situation through detailed negotiations with the customer to reduce the cost of incompatible documentation and to modify the discount structure. Had the negotiations failed, the company would have declined the business, and would have removed all associated operating costs, so overall profitability would have improved whatever the outcome. However, the negotiations succeeded and served the mutual long-term benefit of both parties.

The review of logistics which followed indicated that 18 warehouses, located correctly, could replace the existing network of 60, and would lead to a saving of £13 million a year in operating costs. One of the new sites coincided with that of an existing location. However, even when converted from a single to a three-shift operation, it could not cope with the required throughput of orders. Examination of the profitability of the different stomer types in the areas to be served by the new warehouse revealed a ticular market segment which generated a great deal of work in proportion to gross margin. By actively encouraging these customers to switch their business to competitors, it was possible to close eight warehouses and service the remaining, profitable volume through the upgraded existing location. Thus for minimal capital expenditure, profitability was dramatically improved and capital released through the sale of redundant sites.

When are activity-based techniques not appropriate for commercial decision support?

Change for its own sake can be counter-productive. It is therefore as important to understand when the use of activity-based decision support techniques are likely to be inappropriate as when they are.

The greater the direct labour content of a product and the lower the variability, variety, complexity and change in the product range or customer base, the less likely it is that the results of an ABC approach will produce product costs significantly different from those of a conventional approach.

In environments where there is either little variability between the behaviour of different customers, or in the method of either production or processing, or where direct labour is the dominant element of cost, the resulting inaccuracy of conventional systems may not be significant. Unfortunately this is not often the case.

Summary

The purpose of activity based *costing* (ABC) – as opposed to activity based *management* (ABM) – is to develop better costs and profitability information and analysis to support commercial decisions. These include portfolio, pricing, margin management and customer access (micromarketing) decisions.

Alongside research into customer needs, ABC provides the opportunity to understand the nature of trading relationships. Through analytical techniques such as 'hook curves' and decision grids, management can initiate focused action to improve productivity, re-engineer customer relationships, model competitor profitability and develop sound commercial strategy.

CHAPTER 7

ABCM to support resource management and change

We are going to win and the industrial West is going to lose out: there's nothing much you can do about it, because the reasons for failure are within yourself... for you, the essence of management is getting the ideas out of the heads of the bosses into the hands of labour ... for us, the core of management is precisely the act of mobilising and pulling together the intellectual resources of all employees . . . only by drawing on the combined brainpower of all its employees can a firm face up to the turbulence and constraints of today's environment

Konosuke Matsushita

In the last chapter we focused on ABCM in commercial decision making – that part of our ABCM framework that supports business *positioning*, or 'doing the right things'. Here, we turn our attention to *capability*, or 'doing them right', which is concerned with resource management and the management of change.

We have already observed that nobody intentionally does things wrong – 'I think I'll make a few mistakes today, for the hell of it'. (Fraud and malice are a separate issue, but they are not mistakes: they are deliberate.) In every organisation, however, things do go wrong. Since nobody intended this, the question of *why* things go wrong is not a trivial one. Understanding activities provides an essential first step in answering it.

Types of activity

Not all activities add equal value. It is clearly of more value, for example, to be selling a customer a new product or service than to be raising a credit note because the company failed to deliver the customer's last order. However, to describe activities as 'value added' and 'non-value added' does little to improve understanding. Many activities do not 'add value', but are necessary in order to enable 'value-adding' activities to occur.

A more useful categorisation of activities is illustrated in Figure 40.

Figure 40 Types of activity

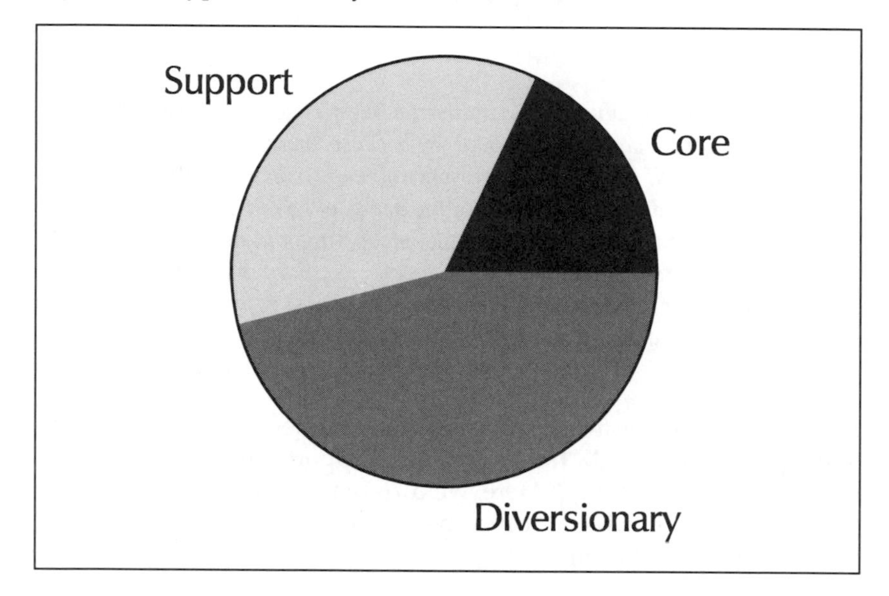

- *Core* activities are those which add value to the business by meeting both customer needs and the company's objectives. Selling a new product or service is therefore a core activity. It also makes use of the salesperson's specialist skills.
- *Support* activities are those which enable core activity to take place: using the above example, the salesperson's time spent travelling to the customer is a support activity. Likewise, activities such as filing and arranging meetings are necessary support activities.
- *Diversionary* activities are those which add cost, but no value. They happen because people are diverted from core or support activity. If the salesperson has to visit the customer to explain why the last

delivery was incomplete or late, the visit is diversionary, as is the travel to get there.

Much diversionary activity masquerades as core activity – for example, the activity of raising credit notes is seen as essential. Indeed it is, because the customer must be refunded the money he is owed. But it adds no value, merely cost. *Core activity is important,* while *diversionary activity is urgent.*

Figure 41 illustrates the case of the marketing department of a contract research and development organisation.

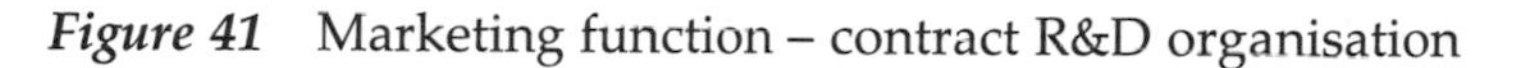

Figure 41 Marketing function – contract R&D organisation

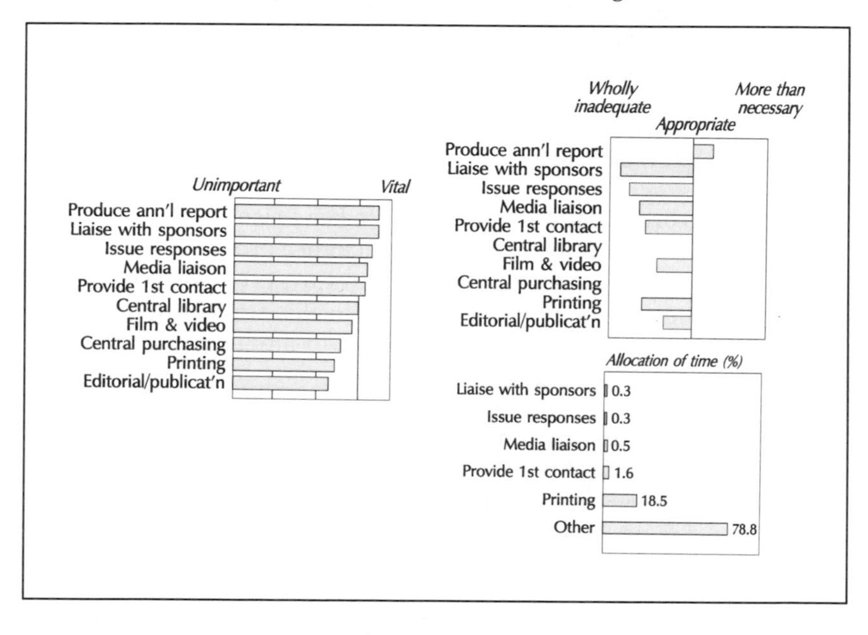

The two upper charts show the results of an internal customer needs survey. The first shows the importance attached to the different activities of the department by its customers – the managers of the research functions; the second shows their perception of the department's performance against each of the activities – not a very positive assessment.

The lower chart shows an analysis of the time spent on various activities within the marketing department. The reason for poor performance on the key activities is now clear: the staff in the department were spending very little time on them. Four-fifths of their time was spent on 'other' activities – *diversionary* activities.

Nobody in the department deliberately ignored their core activities. They were obliged to undertake a variety of diversionary activities because something, somewhere had gone wrong, and it fell to them to put it right.

The classification of activities in this way is therefore *not* a comment on *individual* performance. Its purpose is to reveal where working processes are failing. The important point about diversionary activity is that its cause usually lies elsewhere in the organisation – that is, elsewhere in a cross-functional business process. The issue is to understand the root cause of diversionary activity, and to eliminate it.

Business processes

Activities in an organisation are not undertaken in isolation: something, such as a request for information or a customer order, triggers them. The activity generates an output, which in turn prompts action from others. Activities that are linked together in this way form a *business process*. Business processes are the lifeblood of any organisation: their summation defines its operations.

Business processes are invariably cross-functional. Diversionary activity is usually driven by something elsewhere in the process: an incomplete delivery may be caused by a failure anywhere in the logistics process, from an incorrect part number from an out-of-date catalogue to a shop-floor scheduling error.

Process failures act like viruses. Just as viruses occupy living cells that lack immunity to them, multiplying rapidly and transmitting infection, so 'viruses' live and multiply in weak business processes. They spread throughout the process, infecting other parts of the organisation, and diverting them into wasted effort – chasing parts or information, correcting errors, checking work already done, raising credit notes, apologising [illegible]

A country-wide white goods chain found that 30 per cent of the documents generated in its high street showrooms contained significant errors. The virus spread from the showrooms to regional offices, where staff were responsible for stockholding and installation. Some documents contained incorrect customer information, causing wasted journeys to install equipment. Others contained incorrect stock codes, delaying delivery to the customer.

The virus infected head office, where the customers' accounts were maintained, and where the marketing department needed correct coding to maintain a marketing database.

The virus was causing people to take corrective action at every point in the supply chain to the customer – diversionary activity that was costing it almost £5 million a year. Ultimately, the virus also infected the customers, who were exposed to the failure of the business to supply the goods they ordered at the time agreed in the showroom.

The failures were caused by the design of the process, not by sloppy work. In a complex sale involving loan financing, insurance, maintenance agreement, and installation arrangements, the customer's name and address were required on as many as six different forms. The forms themselves were poorly laid out, and there were no instructions on how they should be filled in. Not surprisingly errors abounded, particularly when the showrooms were busy. In the regional offices people tried their best to correct errors, but the process constantly defeated them. Line management fought fires, but were unable to make changes outside their own departments – their own sphere of influence.

Diversionary activity is therefore a symptom of process failure. Identifying and eliminating the root cause of process failure will remove the need for, and cost of, the diversionary activity that exists to correct the failure.

In the case study above, there was a two-stage solution to the problem – the first eliminated the primary cause of diversionary activity, which was poor design of the forms being used in 650 high street showrooms. This eliminated half of the £5 million diversionary activity in regional and head offices. The second stage was the fundamental redesign of the process itself.

Process re-engineering/redesign

The purpose of redesigning a business process is not simply to eliminate diversionary activity, but to make a step change in the way in which the process delivers service to customers and benefit to the business. This involves addressing all types of activity, by:

- enhancing core activity;
- undertaking new core activity (providing new services);
- where appropriate, relocating activity to different parts of the organisation;
- making support activity as efficient and effective as possible;
- actively preventing diversionary activity.

> *At the white goods chain, process redesign involved the installation of a point-of-sale computer system. The system completely eliminated the requirement to complete manual forms: having prompted the customer once for his or her name, address and other relevant information, the system generated all the necessary legal documentation for finance and maintenance agreements. It also checked the availability of stock, immediately allocated it to the customer and scheduled and confirmed the date and time of delivery within a two-hour window. The system also performed credit scoring and initiated the necessary payment processes.*
>
> *The result was that activities that had been carried out in central functions (credit checking, generation of legal documents, and so forth) were now relocated to the showroom, helped by a computer system designed to prevent errors.*
>
> *Showroom staff time was released for new selling activity, and the new credit scoring activity carried out mainly by the computer system reduced the incidence of bad debt. The support activity of maintaining the marketing database was now automated, which in turn enabled new (core) marketing initiatives based on up-to-date, complete information.*

All these changes generated quantified benefits throughout the organisation, by causing measurable changes to activities – changing the *mix* of core, support and diversionary in favour of core at the expense of diversionary. However, the main benefit to the business arose not from these changes, but from the dramatic improvement in customer service. The organisation changed from being reactive to customer demand and complaint, to being proactive in meeting customer needs and generating new marketing and selling opportunities for the business.

Cost cutting and cost reduction

It is still common practice for senior management to cut costs by insisting on an across-the-board percentage cut in budget. This is frankly inept. It assumes that waste and diversionary activity allocate themselves in equal proportions to all functions in the organisation.

There is a subtle but critically important difference between 'cost cutting' and 'cost reduction'. 'Cost cutting' refers to any management practice aimed at removing costs rapidly, which often involves people losing their jobs. By contrast, 'cost reduction' describes a *continuous* process of reducing unit costs. By improving profitability, cost reduction is a means of *creating* jobs. The logic is straightforward: unless a company continually reduces the cost of developing, producing and delivering products and services to meet the needs of its customers, it will become uncompetitive.

Furthermore, cost reduction should not be seen as a 'management' practice, but one that all staff are engaged in. Understanding activity costs, the nature of core, support and diversionary activities, and the interrelationship of activities to form business processes, create a powerful means of encouraging a minimum cost culture.

Process management

The nature of accountability

Most organisations are functional hierarchies. Business re-engineering almost invariably challenges this conventional structure, encouraging the establishment of multi-disciplinary teams, breaking down the barriers between organisational units, and minimising levels of supervision and management.

In Chapter **2** we pointed out that one of the most significant weaknesses of conventional management accounts and budgeting systems is their focus on the cost centre or department, not on cross-functional processes.

Why do we have cost centres? The answer usually has something to do with 'accountability'. Senior management wants to hold managers 'accountable' for results, and the way results are conventionally measured is by profit and loss. Is it not logical therefore to treat each department as having its own mini-P&L? If every department meets its budget, the whole enterprise will succeed.

We have already observed that this ignores the fact that business processes are cross-functional. We contend that *cost and income are secondary*, because cost is the *consequence* of resource decisions, and income is the *consequence* of business processes that deliver products and services to customers. It follows that to manage costs effectively, the requirement is to improve the quality of resource decisions; to increase income, the requirement is to improve business processes.

Since activities consume resources and convert them to output, and since processes are linked activities, understanding of activities is fundamental to effective process management.

As a starting point for examination of the potential of ABCM in providing better information to support process management, we return to the example of a purchasing department that we used in Chapters **2** and **3**. The company was a supplier of equipment mainly to the Ministry of Defence.

We have already pointed out that this cost centre budget statement is more remarkable for what it omits than what it tells us. There are only two items of information on this statement that are partially useful to the departmental manager who is trying to make improvements:

Expense	*£000pa*
People costs	778
Travel and entertainment	130

These are the only two elements of the manager's departmental budget over which he or she has *direct* control. All other elements are fragments of other departments' costs, and we shall assume that the whole cost of these elements is being tackled in the same way where they are being incurred.

Figure 42 Typical departmental budget statement – purchasing department, engineering company

Description	£000
Salaries	665
Associated staff costs	113
Total staff costs	778
Travel and entertainment	130
Staff restaurant	18
Telephone	14
Stationery	9
Premises – rent	65
– rates	13
Equipment – maintenance	17
– depreciation	7
Utilities	11
Insurance	5
Management fee	45
Central computer charge	27
Total non-staff costs	361
TOTAL	1,139

This information, as it stands, is profoundly irrelevant. Since the purchasing department has employed people (a resource decision) the information that they cost money is neither surprising nor useful. Nor, incidentally, is it necessary to provide the information monthly. Having employed them to do a job, it is also unsurprising that they need to travel and entertain.

However, taking these two elements of cost and allocating them to the *activities* that these staff undertake provides the information in Figure 43.

Figure 43 Purchasing department activity costs

	Staff Costs £'000s	*Travel & Ent Costs £'000s*	*Purchasing Department £'000s*
Assessment of requirements	20	-	20
Requisitioning process	61	-	61
Approvals	12	-	12
Supplier intelligence	5	1	6
Buying negotiations	112	33	145
Progress chasing	116	-	116
Data input	97	-	97
' Noise '	134	55	189
Direct Purchasing costs	**557**	**89**	**646**
Management & admin	111	31	142
Communications	62	7	69
Other	48	3	51
Indirect Purchasing Costs	**221**	**41**	**262**
Apparent Cost of Purchasing	**778**	**130**	**908**

This is immediately useful, because it enables management to start asking questions that are relevant to making improvements. What is 'noise'? This is responding to queries from engineers who need purchased components and raw material for the lethal devices they are building for the MoD. 'Progress chasing' is the time spent by the purchasing department staff ringing up and chasing suppliers. Why is relatively so little time devoted to assessing requirements?

Purchasing is a *process*. There are therefore 'purchasing' activities that take place in other departments of the business, analysis of which gives the following *process* costs:

Figure 44 Purchasing process activity costs

	Purchasing Department £'000s	*All Other Departments £'000s*	*Total Cost of Purchasing Process £'000s*
Assessment of requirements	20	192	212
Requisitioning process	61	203	264
Approvals	12	84	96
Supplier intelligence	6	23	29
Buying negotiations	145	255	400
Progress chasing	116	137	253
Data input	97	-	97
'Noise'	189	120	309
Direct Purchasing costs	**646**	**1014**	**1660**
Management & admin	142	?	142
Communications	69		69
Other	51		51
Indirect Purchasing Costs	**262**	?	**262**
Real Cost of Purchasing	**908**	+ MIN **1014**	**1922**

Clearly, more purchasing activity takes place *outside* the purchasing department than within it – including assessment of requirements by engineers. Throughout the process more than half a million pounds a year is spent on 'noise' and progress chasing. Classification by the staff themselves of core, support and diversionary activity produces the breakdown shown in Figure 45.

Figure 45 Core, support and diversionary activities in the purchasing process

	Purchasing Process £'000s	Type of Activity: Core £'000s	Support £'000s	Diversionary £'000s
Assessment of requirements	212	212		
Requisitioning process	264		264	
Approvals	96			96
Supplier intelligence	29	29		
Buying negotiations	400	400		
Progress chasing	253			253
Data input	97	97		
` Noise '	309			309
Direct Purchasing costs	**1660**	**738**	**264**	**658**
Management & admin	142			142
Communications	69		69	
Other	51		51	
Indirect Purchasing Costs	**262**	**-**	**120**	**142**
Real Cost of Purchasing	**1922**	**738**	**384**	**800**

The main opportunities for improvement lie in tackling the causes of diversionary activity. But this obviously cannot be the responsibility of a single departmental manager. *Eliminating the root causes of diversionary activity requires cooperation between functions in the process*. This means we must challenge what we mean by 'accountability'.

We need to distinguish between *method* accountability, which is vertical, and *process* accountability, which is horizontal. A departmental manager can normally be said to have method accountability – that is, control over *how* the work is undertaken, but limited or no control over the volumes and service levels being demanded: these are dictated by the needs of internal or external customers.

Both method and process accountability are needed to achieve *total* cost accountability. It requires internal cooperation supported by useful information about customer needs, volumes, capacity, resources, activities, outputs, service levels, and variation. It does *not* mean cross-charging, which never contains this type of information.

If we apply this to our example of a purchasing department, the purchasing manager has method accountability for the unit costs of his department: this includes developing good buying practice, developing relationships with suppliers, monitoring price trends, supplier intelligence, supplier quality assurance, and so forth – the core activities of the department. Only by cooperating with other managers in the purchasing process, who share process accountability, can the causes of diversionary activity in the process be eliminated.

Process management does not necessarily conflict with the need for functions. It requires a change to the concept of accountability. This needs more than a will to work together: cooperation must be well informed. Process managers need visibility of the process, and measures of process output.

Process visibility

Process mapping is a simple, effective way to provide process visibility. Figure 46 illustrates a process map.

A process map can show:

- the 'cast of characters' – which departments are involved in the process;
- the main activities;
- the decision points – where much diversionary activity often takes place, such as checking for errors;
- the feedback loops – where the process crosses back across functional boundaries, frequently for rework or queries;
- the number of 'hand-offs', or steps in the process;
- the process time – time taken by activities, and delays between activities as the process crosses departmental boundaries;
- the geographic separation of activities in the process.

Figure 46 Process mapping

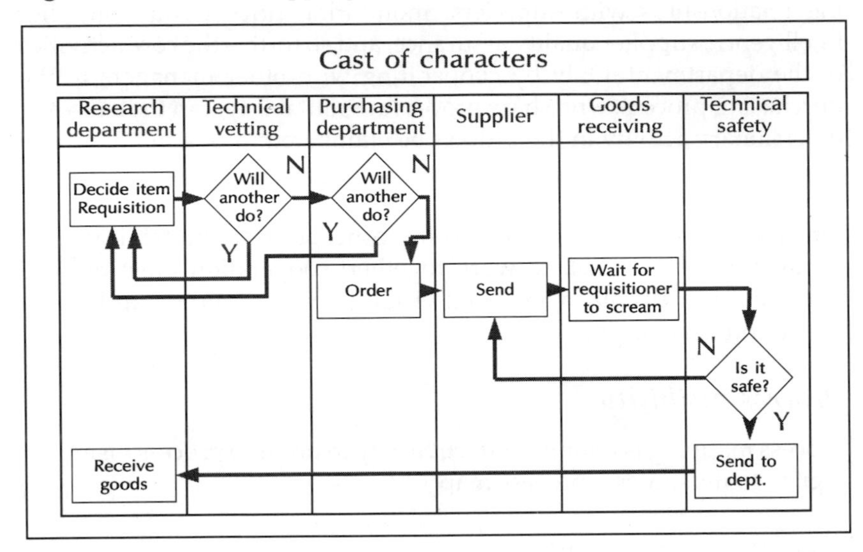

The exercise of mapping processes for the first time is instructive. Having drawn an initial map, the next step is to assemble the cast of characters – the managers of the departments involved – and hold a validation meeting. This group is the process management team. In addition to correcting the map, the meeting invariably initiates a lively discussion and debate about *why* things happen the way they do.

When activity data is then collected, identifying which activities are core, support and diversionary, the pursuit of process failure can begin.

Well-informed process management also requires measures of output and process performance.

Measuring output and process performance

We have observed that conventional management accounts are concerned primarily with measuring input costs, or resources that are *supplied*. Activities convert resources into output. It is therefore important to be able to measure the output of activities and processes from the perspective of the customer.

Two rather different examples of output, or process measurement will serve to illustrate what they are, and to highlight the limitations of conventional management accounts in providing information that will help management improve processes.

Figure 47 shows the actual expenditure profile for the purchasing department we have been examining.

Figure 47 Budget and actual expenses profile – purchasing department

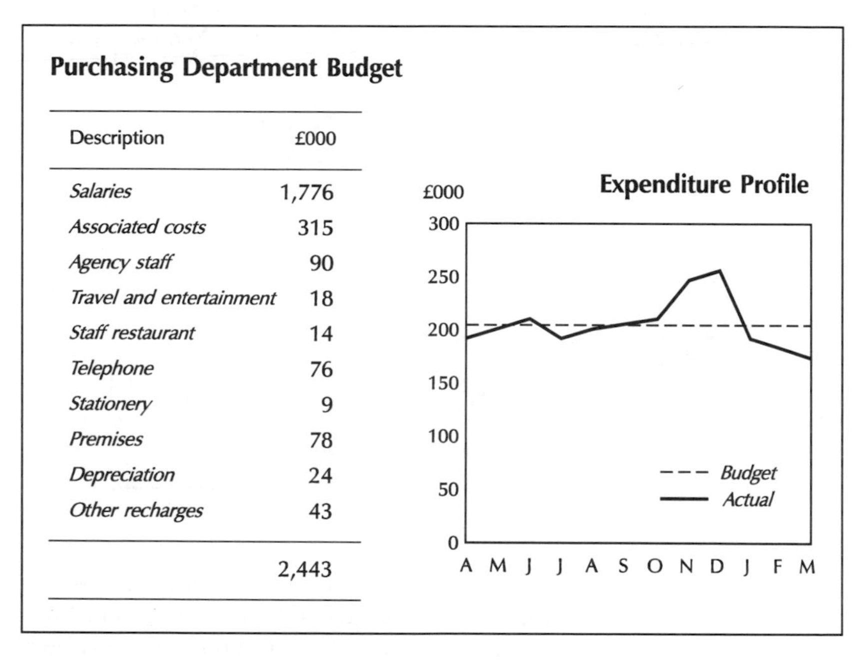

Purchasing Department Budget

Description	£000
Salaries	1,776
Associated costs	315
Agency staff	90
Travel and entertainment	18
Staff restaurant	14
Telephone	76
Stationery	9
Premises	78
Depreciation	24
Other recharges	43
	2,443

Historically, annual departmental expenditure had always been within 5 per cent of budget. In the last year, for which the expenditure profile is shown above, total expenditure was less than 0.5 per cent below budget. This exemplary performance resulted annually in warm praise for the purchasing manager, accompanied by a bonus.

The expenditure profile shows the budget (the same for every month) and actual monthly expenditure. The profile of variances was due to the manager's annual practice of using agency staff before Christmas to deal with a backlog of work, then reducing staff numbers sharply in the New Year to ensure that the department came in on budget.

The company was a supplier to the Ministry of Defence. At the time most contracts were on a cost-plus basis, with stage payments for completed work. Two output measures were produced for the purchasing process, shown in Figure 48.

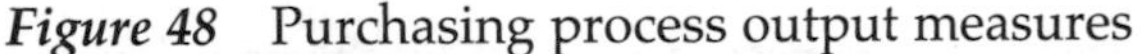

Figure 48 Purchasing process output measures

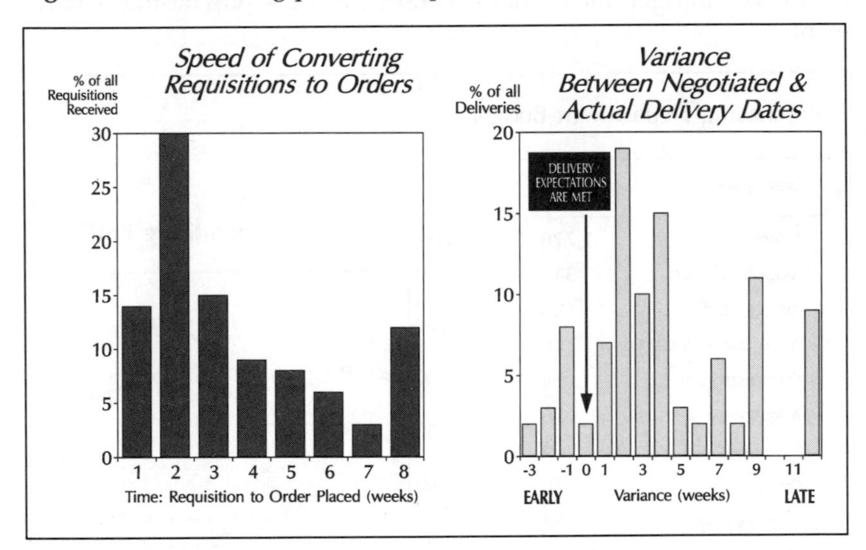

The measures reflect the performance of the purchasing process as perceived by its internal customers. The first shows the length of time taken to convert purchase requisitions to orders, and the second shows the profile of delivery from suppliers against the agreed delivery date. In both cases, delays could be both extensive (up to eight weeks!), and *unpredictable.*

The resulting cash-flow problems and consequential losses from failing to obtain timely MoD payments for completed work were far more significant costs to the business than a small budget overrun in the purchasing department.

The measures pointed to the action needed – reduction in both lead times and variability in the requisitioning process, and development of relationships with suppliers to ensure consistent on-time deliveries.

The output measures led to examination of many other issues, including, for example:

- policies on competitive tendering as a cause of delay and variability in converting requisitions to tenders;
- the practice of buying on price alone (lowest tender), with secondary regard for delivery performance and quality;
- the role of functions outside purchasing in the purchasing process – for example, delays and costs driven by inadequate specification of requirements;
- the fact that more activity related to the purchasing process took place *outside* purchasing than within it.

The second example of output measures is that of a telephone switchboard. Figure 49 gives a profile of calls received through a switchboard in a retail bank over a working week, showing the split between calls taken by the operators and direct dial inward (DDI) calls, where the caller can bypass the switchboard by calling the internal extension directly. It also shows the percentage of operators' calls that were answered within 10 seconds.

Figure 49 Telephone answering statistics – bank

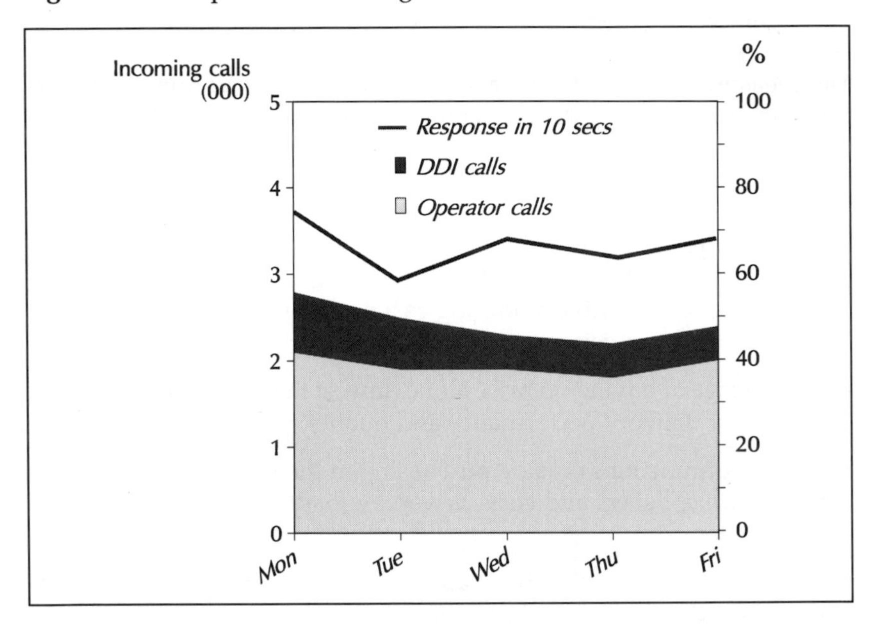

The measures raised a number of issues:

- It is probable that a significant proportion of the calls taken by operators are from people calling the bank for the first time, and that this would therefore provide their first impression of the bank. Increasing operator capacity to improve response would therefore be an important improvement to customer service.
- The 'target' response of 90 per cent of calls to be answered within 10 seconds was not being achieved: if action could be taken to increase the number of directly dialled (DDI) calls, operator time would be released to improve response.
- Once the target of 90 per cent was consistently achieved, the target could be changed, giving continuous improvement. In any case, knowledge of the *actual* service level was more important than the target.
- It was possible to know the cost of the particular service level being achieved, and to predict the cost of improving the service.

Process and output measures such as these can be seen as measures of process health, or *pulse points*. They are also often referred to as *key performance indicators* (KPIs). However, it is important to stress that they are not intended to be measures of *personal* performance. The purpose of output measures is to measure *process* performance from the perspective of the customer, for the benefit of both management and the staff working in the process. Much of their value is the extent to which they clarify process accountability, and highlight cross-functional dependencies and the need for cooperation.

Activity based budgeting

Definition of budgeting

> *Budgeting is the method by which an organisation allocates resources to business processes, to establish the necessary capability to produce forecast outputs and to invest in the future.*

If we accept this as a useful definition of budgeting, or what budgeting ought to be, then *by definition it is not a method of cost control*. The problem is that in the absence of a better system of cost management, organisations use budgeting as a surrogate method of cost control.

Effective cost management is based on understanding processes and activity costs; core, support and diversionary activity; volumes, and trends, cyclicality and variation; service levels; and cause-and-effect through cost drivers. This is ABCM.

Budgeting should be the *consequence* of an effective cost management process. The link between cost management and budgeting is defined by Kaplan's 'fundamental equation of ABC' given in Chapter **4**:

Cost of resources supplied = Cost of resources used + Cost of excess capacity

Budgeting should be used to decide the left-hand side of this equation: the resources to be supplied, such as people, equipment, and premises. Cost management is in the right-hand side of the equation, since *resources used* are activities with current methods .

ABC defines cost drivers for activities. It is therefore possible to use ABC as the basis for developing those elements of the budget that have cost drivers. At cost centre level, therefore:

Forecast cost driver volume X Cost driver unit cost = Forecast activity cost

For example, the cost driver for supplier negotiations in a purchasing department may be the number of new component designs. If the cost driver unit cost is £2,360, and the forecast volume of new component designs is 30, the forecast activity cost for supplier negotiations will be:

Forecast cost driver volume X Cost driver unit cost = Forecast activity cost

$$30 \times £2{,}360 = £70{,}800$$

The budget may or may not include excess capacity – this would be an explicit budget assumption.

Developing budgets in this way eliminates many of the weaknesses of conventional approaches: the basis for planning resources is objective data on cost driver volumes and activity unit costs.

Cost driver unit costs can be varied by the extent to which diversionary activity can be eliminated, and different ways of working implemented. In other words, *the outcome of business change initiatives can be quantified and built into the budgeting process.*

Summary

Not all activities add equal value, and it is therefore useful to classify activities as *core, support* or *diversionary*. Because diversionary activity is mainly driven by process failure elsewhere in the organisation, improvement depends on tracking back to the root cause of the failure.

Activities are not undertaken in isolation – they form part of cross-functional business processes. Re-engineering processes is a means of improving customer service at lower cost.

While 'cost cutting' involves step change and job loss, cost reduction is a continuous process of improving profitability, which creates jobs.

Output measures reflect the performance of business processes from the perspective of the customer, and thereby the value for money spent on the resources.

Activity based budgeting builds budgets on the basis of planned output, rather than as an extrapolation of historical inputs.

CHAPTER 8

Implementation issues

There is nothing more difficult to execute, nor more dubious of success, nor more dangerous to administer than to introduce a new order of things; for he who introduces it has all those who profit from the old order as enemies, and he has only lukewarm allies in all those who might profit from the new. This . . . stems . . . partly from the sceptism of men, who do not truly believe in new things unless they have actually had personal experience of them.

Niccolo Machiavelli

The difference between successful implementation of ABCM and failure is not merely a matter of technique and technical experience. It is the consequence of a rigorous implementation process which takes account of a wide range of considerations. These are summarised in Figure 50, and are explored further in this chapter.

'Thoughtware'

'Thoughtware' describes all the issues which need to be carefully thought through at an early stage of any project aimed at developing an activity-based decision-support model.

Figure 50 Components of an ABCM decision support project

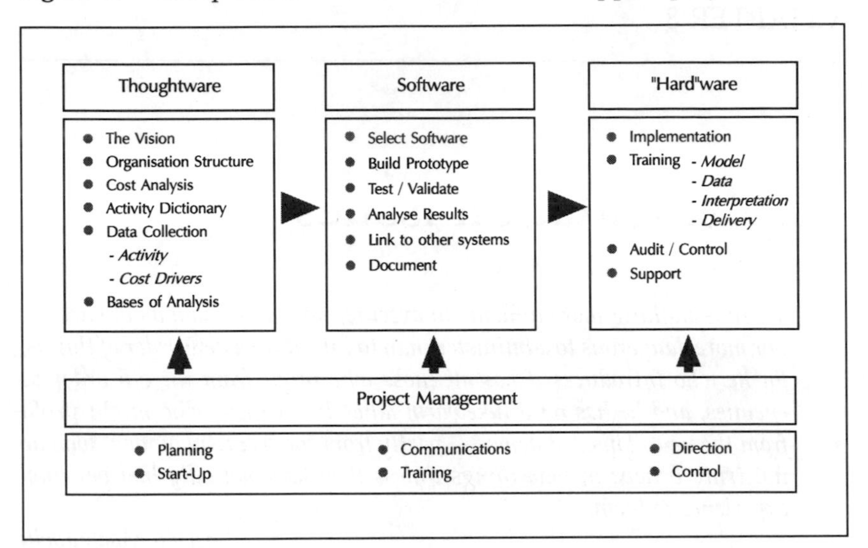

The vision

Our ABCM framework, reproduced in Figure 51, describes the variety of initiatives which can benefit from a well constructed activity database.

While in theory, all of these possibilities could be pursued concurrently, it would be difficult to do them all well.

Semantics complicate matters. The three letter acronyms (TLAs) in use, such as ABC, ABM and ABB, hold different meanings for different people. We use the term *ABCM* as an umbrella to include all forms of activity based initiatives. It is therefore important to ensure that senior management have a clear, shared view of the expected outcome of an ABCM initiative.

It helps if the project can be set in the strategic context of the organisation so that management and staff can see how it contributes to the overall development of the organisation. In Chapter **3** we described how strategy can be explained in terms of *positioning* and *capability*.

Figure 51 ABCM framework

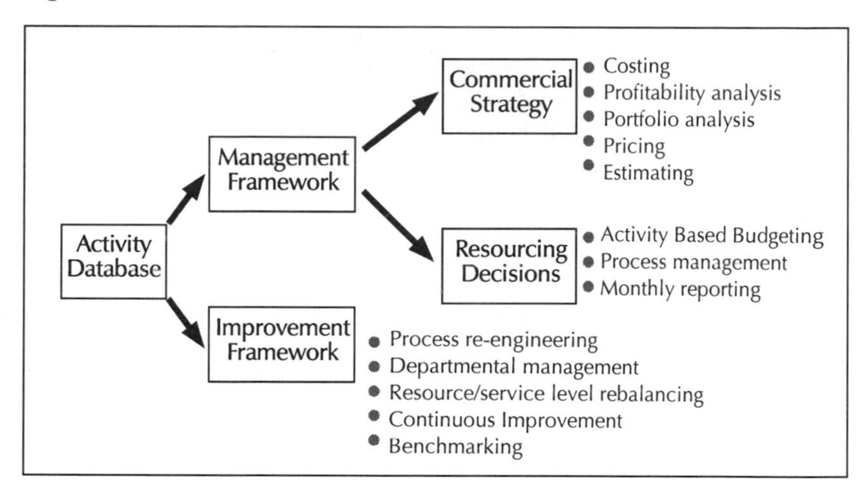

Activity based *costing* techniques strongly support a wide range of commercial and strategic *positioning* decisions such as costing, estimating, pricing, profit margin management, product and customer portfolio analysis, mix and channel, make or buy, and marketing and strategy. It is important to note that none of these is directly related to issues of efficiency and effectiveness, such as how individual activities are undertaken.

By contrast, activity based *management* techniques fall into the two broad categories of resource management and change management, or improvement, both of which support *capability* decisions. Resourcing decisions are largely related to the cost-effective management of capacity and service levels, including budgeting, and to process management. Improvement decisions relate to the enhancement of efficiency and effectiveness through techniques such as continuous improvement, resource rebalancing, cost reduction and business process re-engineering.

Once the purpose of the exercise has been identified and agreed by senior management, it should be stated clearly and used to drive the focus of the exercise.

Consistency

There are two aspects to the issue of consistency. The first concerns the definition of activity levels, which we discussed in Chapter **5**. If maximum flexibility is required, activities should be defined *from the top down*, each level of detail being a disaggregation of the level immediately above it.

The second concerns consistency at a given level of detail, particularly between different areas within a medium or large organisation. Here it is often helpful to prepare a provisional dictionary of activities and cost drivers as a guide to those undertaking the implementation.

Software

Activity based techniques require significant data manipulation in all but the most simple applications.

In the early 1980s the manipulation of activity databases was a significant technical problem, in some cases to the point where it was a constraint on what would be achieved. The options then were simple; a Lotus spreadsheet, or a mainframe and programmers. Developments since then have been dramatic both in terms of hardware and software. It is now possible to buy ABCM-specific PC-based software with the necessary power and user-friendliness for the largest ABCM applications.

ABC software suppliers have recognised the potential of the market for ABCM-specific software and are competing strongly to understand and meet the needs of prospective users. However, this part of the software market is still in a state of rapid development. It is important to talk directly to existing users of the competing software packages to understand their practical experience.

'Hard'ware

Unless the results of an activity-based costing model directly influence the commercial, strategic and resource decisions of management, then the effort will have been wasted. A successful outcome hinges on the following:

- *Management commitment*: this is most often won by ensuring that senior and middle managers, and staff, understand the fundamental *need* which the implementation is there to support. It is also important for people to recognise the fit with other initiatives.
- *Ownership*: as the implementation progresses it is essential that all involved understand how the model has been constructed, and believe that it provides a sufficiently fair reflection of *their* part of the cost structure, and what drives it.
- *Delivered benefits*: it is of equal importance to involve the *users* of the activity-based information. If they understand its origins and its meaning they will be better equipped to interpret it correctly. Because the information will be new to them, it is often helpful to prepare case study material to illustrate how best use of the information can be made, and to define its limitations. A participative workshop environment is also helpful as this allows decision-makers to share the learning with others.
- *Elimination of threat*: if decision-makers at any level of an organisation, feel that they will be penalised for decisions that hindsight shows to be flawed, they will resist change.
- *Feedback*: particularly where the decisions are frequent, such as in estimating, pricing or resource allocation decisions, it is an important part of the learning process that the consequences are quickly identified and fed back to the decision-makers. This reinforces the benefits of the transition to the new approach, and minimises the risks. As evidence of success grows, effort should be made to communicate this widely within the organisation.

Project management

The board needs to act as a steering group for an ABCM project, because of its cross-functional implications. The project team should be drawn from all functions in the business, with a core of full-time members, and a full-time, senior project manager who has the respect of all.

In many organisations there is a wide variation in perception of the issues facing the business, and how to address them. It is therefore important to understand these perceptions and play them back to senior management *before* the project is started so that any serious difficulties can be identified and resolved.

The nature of the project will determine whether all parts of the organisation should be included at the same time, or not. Normally it is better to include all areas within the scope as a matter of course. However, certain types of analysis – such as customer profitability analysis – are critically dependent on this.

If the intention is to embed an activity based approach into the fabric of how an organisation routinely manages itself and makes commercial decisions, it is important to establish a recognised *centre of excellence*. Ideally, the core project team forms the basis of this group.

External support

While external consultants have specialist experience and knowledge, it is internal staff who know most about the organisation and its business. We believe the ideal approach is an internal team facilitated by consultants, whose main responsibility should be the transfer of expertise to the internal team.

The role of the finance function

The finance function has a particularly important role to play in the implementation of activity based techniques. Accountants are well positioned both to understand the financial and commercial imperatives which drive the need for the initiative in the first place, and to contribute numerate and analytical skills. As experienced providers of information in the organisation they are also well placed to become the centre of excellence for activity based techniques.

However, the perception that ABCM is a finance function initiative should be avoided, in order to encourage ownership by line management. One of the great advantages of ABCM is its ability to 'translate' financial language into the language of management. If some of the credibility of the finance function has been eroded in recent years by the weaknesses of conventional management accounting and costing systems, ABCM provides the opportunity to restore it, and to develop a proactive role in business performance measurement.

Summary

Successful implementation of ABCM depends firstly on establishing a clear purpose for the exercise, for which the positioning and capability model provides a useful framework. Appropriate software offerings need to be examined carefully in the light of the purpose and requirement.

Above all, management commitment and ownership at all levels are critical to success. The change invariably requires sustained education and effective communication and feedback. This is all the more important since the scope of an ABCM project is almost always the whole organisation, requiring changes to both individual and corporate behaviours.

The finance function has a pivotal role to play, but ABCM should not be regarded as a functional initiative.

CHAPTER 9

The way forward

The past beyond management; the future is within its grasp.
Robin Bellis-Jones

In Chapter **1**, we said that activity based cost management is concerned with two fundamentals: 'doing the right things', and 'doing them right'.

***Figure* 52** ABCM The value of

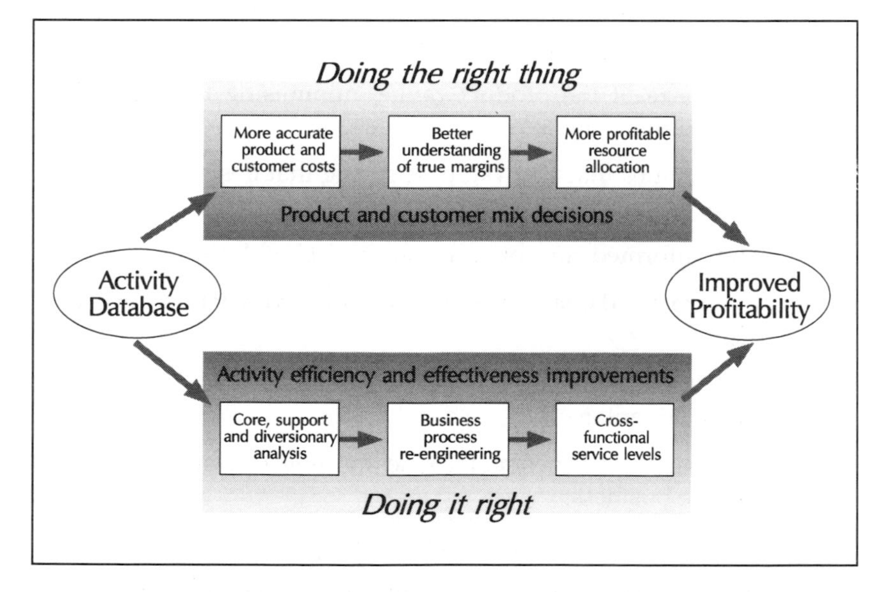

Despite its name, activity based cost management is not an accounting technique: it is *part of the management process*. It speaks the language of management, and supports the decisions that managers have to make. It makes visible the fundamentals of what drives the business. It does this in such a way that opportunities to improve are continuously exposed and quantified. It removes the problem of 'failure to take action because management did not know that a change was needed, nor what it was worth'.

It does, however, require management to accept that good management information does not depend on the historical numbers in the financial accounts. Instead, management needs the knowledge that such numbers alone cannot provide. There is no longer any reason for hidden profits and losses to remain hidden.

Recognition of the costs of activities and what drives them provides a powerful incentive for management to:

- recognise the way in which customers, the channels by which they are served, and individually how they choose to behave directly affect the cost structure of the business;
- control the size of the product range, minimising the number of products and their rate of change;
- focus on activities that add value, ensuring that design, production and service are 'right first time';
- seek better informed control of design/redesign decisions;
- avoid the errors and distortions often found in conventional accounting systems;
- have confidence in making commercial decisions that lead to sound competitive advantage;
- recognise the cross-functional cause-and-effect relationships that underpin the business;
- re-engineer key business processes for competitive advantage;
- develop a better understanding of the costs of complexity, variety and change inherent in both the product- and customer-driven aspects of their business;

- use this understanding to drive the process of continuous improvement.

Managers already know intuitively that these are sound objectives to pursue. What makes the difference is that activity-based decision-support information gives clarity through measurement to the issues involved.

Bibliography

Robin Bellis-Jones	'Customer profitability analysis' *Management Accounting* (Vol 67 No 2 February 1989) p26–28
Michael Bromwich and Alnoor Bhimani	'Management accounting; evolution not revolution' *Chartered Institute of Management Accountants* (1989)
	'Management accounting: pathways to progress' *Chartered Institute of Management Accountants* (1994)
Jan Cobb, John Innes and Falconer Mitchell	'Activity based costing: problems in practice' *Chartered Institute of Management Accountants* (1992)
Robin Cooper	'Does your company need a new cost system?' *Journal of Cost Management for the Manufacturing Industry* (Vol 1 Spring 1987) p45–49
	'Implementing activity-based cost management: moving from analysis to action' *Institute of Management Accountants* (US) (1993)
	'The rise of activity-based costing – part one: what is an activity-based cost system?' *Journal of Cost Management for the Manufacturing Industry* (Vol 2 No 2 Summer 1988) p45–54

'The rise of activity-based costing – part two: when do I need an activity-based cost system?' *Journal of Cost Management for the Manufacturing Industry* (Vol 2 No 3 Fall 1988) p41–48

'The rise of activity-based costing – part three: how many cost drivers do you need and how do you select them?' *Journal of Cost Management for the Manufacturing Industry* (Vol 2 No 4 Winter 1989) p34–46

'The rise of activity-based costing – part four: What do activity-based cost systems look like?' *Journal of Cost Management for the Manufacturing Industry* (Vol 4 No 1 Spring 1990) p32–42

'Implementing an activity-based cost system' *Journal of Cost Management for the Manufacturing Industry* (Vol 4 No 1 Spring 1990) p32–42

'The two-stage procedure in cost accounting: part one' *Journal of Cost Management for the Manufacturing Industry* (Vol 1 Summer 1987) p43–51

'The two-stage procedure in cost accounting: part two' *Journal of Cost Management for the Manufacturing Industry* (Vol 1 Fall 1987) p39–45

'When should you use machine-hour costing?' *Journal of Cost Management for the Manufacturing Industry* (Vol 12 No 1 Spring 1988) p33–39

Robin Cooper and Robert S. Kaplan — *The design of cost management systems: text, cases and readings* (Prentice Hall International 1991)

Develin & Partners — *Freeing the victims* (1990)

Peter F. Drucker — 'The information executives truly need' *Harvard Business Review* (January-February 1995)

Thomas S. Dudick — 'Why SG&A doesn't always work' *Harvard Business School* (Vol 65 No 4 January-February 1987) p30–32, 36

Dr W Edwards Deming — *Out of the Crisis* (Cambridge University Press 1988)

George Foster and Charles T. Horngren — 'Cost accounting and cost management in a JIT environment' *Journal of Cost Management for the Manufacturing Industry* (Vol 1 No 4 Winter 1988) p4–14

'Flexible manufacturing systems: cost management and cost accounting implications' *Journal of Cost Management for the Manufacturing Industry* (Vol 2 Fall 1988) p16–24

Toshiro Hiromoto — 'Another hidden edge – Japanese management accounting' *Harvard Business School* (Vol 88 No 4 1988) p22–24

John Innes and Falconer Mitchell — 'Activity based costing: a review with case studies' *Chartered Institute of Management Accountants* (1991)

'Activity based cost management: a case of study of development and implementation' *Chartered Institute of Management Accountants* (1989)

'Activity based costing in the UK's largest companies' *Chartered Institute of Management Accountants* (1995)

H. Johnson and Robert S. Kaplan	*Relevance lost: the rise and fall of management accounting* (Cambridge MA, Harvard Business School Press, 1987)
Robert S. Kaplan	'Accounting lag: the obsolescence of cost accounting systems' in Kim B. Clark, Robert H. Hayes, Christopher Koenig (eds) *The Uneasy Alliance: managing the productivity-technology dilemma* (Boston, Mass., Harvard Business School Press, 1988) p485
	'Yesterday's accounting undermines production' *Harvard Business Review* (Vol 62 July-August 1984) p95–101
Robert S. Kaplan and B. Maskell	'Relevance regained' *Management Accounting* (Sept 1988)
Thomas B. Lammert and Robert Ehrsam	'The human element: the real challenge in modernizing cost systems' *Management Accounting (USA)* (Vol 69 No 1 July 1987) p32–37
Jeffrey G. Miller Thomas E. Vollmann	'The hidden factory' *Harvard Business Review* (Vol 63 September 1985) p142–50
H. Thomas Johnson	'Activity-based information; a blueprint for world-class management accounting' *Management Accounting (USA)* (Vol 69 No 12 June 1988) p23–30
H. Thomas Johnson and Dennis A. Loewe	'How Weyerhaeuser manages corporate overhead costs' *Management Accounting (USA)* (Vol 69 No 2 August 1987) p20–26
Michael D. Shields and S. Mark Young	'A behavioral model for implementing cost management systems' *Journal of Cost Management for the Manufacturing Industry* (Vol 2 Winter 1989) p17–27

Publication details

Journal of Cost Management for the Manufacturing Industry
Warren, Gorham & Lamong
210 South Street
Boston
Mass. 02111
USA

Management Accounting
The Chartered Institute of Management Accountants
63 Portland Place
London W1N 4AB

Management Accounting Research
The Chartered Institute of Management Accountants
63 Portland Place
London W1N 4AB

Management Accounting (USA)
Institute of Management Accountants
10 Paragon Drive
Montvale
New Jersey 07645-1760
USA

Harvard Business Review
Subscriber Service
PO Box 52623
Boulder
Colorado 80322-2623
USA

For reprints of single articles send orders to:

Dynamic Graphics International
PO Box 25
3950 AA Maam
The Netherlands

UNIVERSITY OF GLAMORGAN
PRIFYSGOL MORGANNWG
Learning Resources
Centre